MW00943143

Third Reality Revealed:

Vision, Persistence, and Inventing

A New Latino Identity

Ernesto Nieto, author

Published by Third Reality Publications
Second Edition

THIRD REALITY REVEALED
Vision, Persistence, and
Inventing a New Latino Identity

Ernesto Nieto

Edited by Alexandria Ocasio-Cortez
Cover Design by Marc S. Nieto, Qobe Group
Spanish Translation by Virginia Roldán-Nieto

Third Reality Publications
Maxwell, Texas

Inquiries and ordering may be addressed to Third Reality Publications, c/o National Hispanic Institute, P.O. Box 220, Maxwell, Texas 78656.

Second Printing, 2014
Digital Edition, 2013
First Printing, 2010
Print ISBN: 978-1499509816

CONTENTS

INTRODUCTION

In the summer of 2001, another intern and I were masters of
ceremonies for the end-of-the week talent show or "Noche
Cultural (cultural night)" at the College of Santa Fe during the
New Mexico Lorenzo De Zavala Youth Legislative Session
(LDZ). Midway through the program Ernesto crept in
through the back door and all we could notice was a huge
smile on his face. I introduced the next act and went to the
back to join him and his wife, and NHI co-founder, Gloria. I
noticed a tear on Gloria's face as she held in her arms a first
edition copy of Third Reality: Crafting a 21st Century Latino
Agenda. Two summers prior I had visited the Lincoln Park
Kinko's in Chicago to print early drafts of the raw text of
what was then called "The NHI Story". That evening as
Gloria held her first edition tightly, Nieto reached into the
box of books, handed me one and said, "Here is yours son."
He opened the cover and signed it.

Among the NHI alumni and community of friends, the
release of that volume created a national buzz. That summer
calls came from throughout the nation to inquire about
getting a copy. Many alumni loved learning the whole story
behind the establishment of the National Hispanic Institute.
Others were intrigued to read all the Ernie and Gloria stories
they had never heard. And others just treasured having the
story of a man whom they admired and an organization they
loved. But in the end, was the book really just an
autobiography?

Amid the excitement, there were critics among the initial pool
of readers that dismissed the book as a poorly written
collection of stories they had heard before. "What was so
important about Ernie's life?" some commented. "It's just a
boring autobiography. What's the big deal?"

Those critiques bothered me. I never believed that the book was written as an autobiography in the first place. Ernie often taught through parables from his own life. He would try to help you look back symbolically to your own memories of family and community history that could guide you or make you consider an alternate life direction. I picked up the book again, this time taking my personal Ernie connection out of the text and allowing myself to connect with a story of self-examination, self-exploration, and self-definition. In the end, Ernie's life was not key. It was his journey and process of self-learning that was the true lesson.

Like many others, I have been anticipating the follow up to this tool for self-discovery. As I moved along in my own journey of examining my identity, my purpose, my role in this world, I often looked to the narrative from Third Reality as a guide that would help me formulate my own questions.

Almost ten years later, life is much more complicated than it was as an intern doing some leisure reading with Ernie's memoir. Six months ago, with a vision that is still being shaped, almost no resources, and faith in oneself, a friend and I set out to create a school for our community through an educational environment that would contribute a new pool of free thinking, asset-driven leaders for decades to come. Arriving here took months of "POOF (proceeding only on faith)" and many travels through my own "Winds of Change".

Third Reality was a compass that kept me examining the type of path I wanted to choose in life. Did I want to continue living a life that was defined by someone else's rules? Did I want to expend energy and time making a positive impact on my community employing the impotent tactics of advocacy and the sluggish models of deficit-based reform? Was I going to continue to accept my life as a citizen of this country as a minority who should wait in line for his turn? Or would I make a shift that would allow my personal reflection of self to be grounded in my identity as a proud American who has the right and power to control, define, and own my future, who can be equally proud to be a citizen of this nation and proud to embrace the rich and cultural traditions of my Latino community?

The echoes of dialogues between Ernesto and his family caused me to begin interviewing my own family more often. It triggered a need to look to my parents, abuelos, cousins, and close friends for advice, counsel, and a reminder of the elements of who I am, what I believe, and what I am capable of. Third Reality kept pushing me through the choice to pursue a "third option"—a life not defined by my parents and friends, nor a life defined by external forces outside of myself. My choice was to live life as I chose to define it. To be Latino, as I define it. To build a collaborative community school that the community defines, shapes, and leads.

Easier said than done. Not even one semester into the establishment of my school, forces are aligned to bring it down. Immediately, my mind races back to the chronicles of NHI's vast challenges. To the moments when Ernie was alone. But, survived. Learned. Continued moving forward. To the memories of my parents taking Christian congregations that started with one or two families. Working together they helped build large collaborative bodies of faith that not only brought the word and hope to countless individuals, but also became the center of community for so many. I saw that with faith, direction, and strong beliefs a vision can truly take form.

My excitement for this new installment is that it takes the reader through a different journey. You will find many of the familiar tones and cast of characters but with a different focus. For if Third Reality was a tale of self-examination and the journey of making a self-guided paradigm shift, this next volume takes along the story of what comes next. This book is a fresh tool for young leaders and learners about living the shift.

Looking back to last February, the decision to live a different life where I was making the rules and attempting to create my own reality was the easy part. It is the next ten to twenty years of my life that will tell us what my third reality will be. What really was my vision if any? There are few examples of leaders that have created or led a movement from an asset view that not only values the intrinsic worth of the individual, but also stands on the beautiful cornucopia of resources that our community possesses. Ernesto's next contribution is one of few guides available to a generation of Latinos attempting to lead differently, create differently, and define Latinidad differently. While Third Reality is a volume of questions and experience that lead to crafting an agenda, this book will also help examine the life cycle of living a new agenda. The resistance. The struggle. The peaks. The valleys. The promise. The inspiration. Seeing the vision materialize. The agenda itself.

I encourage you to use this tool for social analysis as Ernesto's narratives provide an authentic and relevant example of living life on one's own terms where the opportunities are endless if you choose for them to be.

Julio Irving Cotto, M.L.A., NMLDZ '97
Bronx, New York, November 2010

1.

CHALLENGES OF CHANGE

*Living in a self-made reality liberates the person to an existence
of fulfillment, of self-determined purpose,
and of life in a world where one has command of the future.*

As Latinos we have the capacities to give ourselves a
complete cultural and identity make-over in preparation for
an exciting new era, a different time and place in our evolving
journey, and in preparation for an invigorating future. The
past is our past and should respectfully be made of our
collective history and understanding of ourselves. We also,
however, need to put it away, so that we may concentrate on
imagining the new and explore that which is yet to occur in
our thinking. In other words, we are capable of becoming
what we wish to become. Moreover, we may do so in
harmony and balance in ways that give us comfort,
contentment, and a strong sense of direction and purpose.

Little more has to be said about the past except that the social
models that long have been held out as the road to our
success as a community are no longer appropriate alternatives
to our future. In just a few decades, the Latino community
has moved from being a distinct minority to a modern and
dynamic community that reflects the majority of the Western
hemisphere. Indeed, the Latino community is assured,
according to demographers, to become one out of every four
Americans by 2050 with no foreseeable slow down in upward
growth.

Today we come armed with the capacities to lessen the
disconnect that has long existed between a small and more
affluent middle class of Latinos and a much larger working

class. The recognition of value in all Latinos can be established within the Latino com- munity. We cannot afford to risk stagnant growth and discoveries across all areas of endeavor because of old, worn out views that dampen the Latino community's perception of itself. This approach wastes human potential and kills the human capacity to imagine.

We know how to reinvigorate a thinning and depleted leadership infrastructure and regain the spirit of civic engagement that has long held Latinos together. We also have the abilities to increase voter participation and enthuse Latino youth to not only enroll in college in much larger numbers, but also complete their undergraduate degree rates at substantially higher rates.

The question on the table is not one of continuing to assess the condition of the Latino community from a deficit point of view, based on constantly delineating the shortcomings of Latinos against a mainstream metric. This approach and its attendant social measures are no longer applicable or even relevant, given the complexity and makeup of an emerging community whose sheer size and vast untapped human potential has yet to be fully explored and understood from an asset point of view.

Those who assume responsibility for crafting an asset-based social model for Latinos, both in the United States and Latin America, will play a critical role in society as the 21st century unfolds.

In a modern day era, Latinos are not induced to participate in a regressive social experience that assigns little to their human value. Such an experience guarantees them more personal failure than success, and is structured politically and economically to allow only the few to emerge at the top while the majority others are left to toil in the middle and the bottom. The same political playbooks of the past are also no longer needed, along with community leaders' continued use of advocacy and reform as methods of change. These relics of the 1960s no longer serve useful purposes in the modern world except to continue painting Latinos as potential liabilities, rather than the assets they represent to themselves and greater society. Whether or not it is yet fully recognized, a new age of increasingly educated, better-skilled Latino leaders is starting to emerge. More informed and articulate leaders are starting to represent the interests of Latinos in all aspects of community life that range from local to national concerns. They are more adept in the use of modern technology and are certainly better able to strike appropriate balances between the needs of specific ethnic populations and the universal concerns of larger society.

The social paradigms that previously guided Latino leadership, along with their attendant beliefs and practices, are starting to fade. Instead, the design of an altogether new set of beliefs has emerged. This new framework respects custom and tradition, but also heartens Latinos and cuts across nationality with the intent of unlocking a progressive, aggressive, and visionary mindset. These changes are not coming from older and more experienced generations. It is the young women and men that are not yet strapped or paralyzed by fears of past experiences that are giving rise to this new day.

Even this new generation, however, will find themselves caught in the quandary of deciding between the popularized rewards held out by mainstream America and those they wish to shape for themselves. Finding answers and pursuing different possibilities will not come from drawing contrasts between social alternatives. Shaping, forming, and implanting new and different sets of community beliefs to guide the future Latino community will demand a different form of concentration, one that requires long term vigil to imagination, faith, and an enduring will to act as the requirement to ask ourselves new and different questions to guide our future thinking.

For most, the journey will at times be frustrating, but also exciting, exhilarating, and moving. Change is always filled with questions, not to mention attempts to dissuade ourselves from the difficult challenge of going from the predictable and safe to the unpredictable and seemingly unanswerable. This time, however, the discussion of change will neither be an experience that leads us to look outside ourselves nor a process that seeks to intellectually analyze societal issues and challenges. Instead, the task will be one of self-inquiry, a process that occurs inside our individual and collective consciousness. This journey goes within to re-examine and develop the social lenses that inform the beliefs that fashion and determine how we view and interpret the world. It is the act of self-evaluation that we as Latinos are well equipped to perform on ourselves and is vitally needed in order to continue experiencing new results different from those in the past.

In essence, there is no other option. The webbings of past conventional practices are now being replaced with the courage needed to venture into the unknown to re-craft a long overdue identity. We must do so with quiet confidence in our capacities to answer the most difficult of challenges and complex questions.

I can hear my own father, Santos Nieto, telling me: *"Sólo tú puedes elegir qué camino recorrer en la vida. Algunas personas te harán sentir importante, pero sólo por conveniencia. No creas en todo lo que oyes. Sólo tú puedes determinar tu destino. Tu vida no puede basarse en lo que otros digan o prometan. Ese derecho es solamente tuyo."* *"Only you should decide what pathways to follow in life. Others will give you importance, but only for their convenience. Don't believe what you hear. Only you can determine your destiny. You can't base your life on what others say or promise. That right belongs to only you."*

My father would often remind me, *"Tienes que aprender a hacerte buenas preguntas que demanden horas y días de reflexión. Y es sólo el primer paso. En muchos casos no te van a gustar las respuestas o, mejor dicho, las verdades que encontrarás. Pero una vez que sepas, sabrás qué decisiones tomar. Porque la verdad es la verdad. Solamente de esta manera podrás tomar decisiones que concuerden con tu vida espiritual, tus valores y la manera en que quieres vivir. Este proceso de saber hacerte preguntas buenas y profundas es algo que dura toda la vida y la única manera en que puedes llegar a entender quién quieres ser sin importar lo que el resto de la gente diga."* *"What you have to learn is to ask yourself good questions that require hours and days of thinking. That's only the first step. In many cases, you will not like the answers, or, better said, the truths you will find. But once you know them, then you know what decisions to make. Because the truth is the truth. Only this way can you make decisions consistent with your spirituality, your values, and the way you wish to conduct your life. The process of learning to ask yourself good and profound questions is something that will last a lifetime and the only manner through which you will learn to understand what you wish to become, without relying on what the world outside has to say about you."*

Dad's advice always had many implications. Not all his counsel came with complete answers. He didn't tell me, for instance, that learning about myself could be highly confusing, on occasions extremely painful, and often energy draining. He didn't tell me that finding out about myself would involve laying awake in bed at night for hours, peering into a mental darkness of end-less questions and multiple sessions of self-talk. He didn't tell me that change can provoke an inability to act for fear of failure.

There were a few other important points that also were never part of our discussions. My father didn't tell me that change is often a solitary mental journey that can result in a person having to contend with more questions than answers. He didn't inform me that the knowledge and wisdom that comes with changing how we view life is often realized through the experience of taking actions and risks associated with not always being able to predict outcomes. The most important insight gained from my father when discussing this topic was that change did not always have to be associated with learning different ways to achieve goals or solve problems. In his view, the most beneficial and positive results that came from changing ourselves occurred during the process of changing the lives of others.

My father once asked me towards the end, *"¿Qué quieres hacer con tu vida ahora que sabes quién eres y qué quieres llegar a ser, ahora que sabes que todos nacemos y en algún momento dejamos de ser parte de esta vida?"* *"What is it that you wish to do with your life, now that you know who you are and wish to become, now that you know that all of us are born and eventually leave this life?"*

My father rarely spoke about death as a final end, but instead as part of a living and continuous journey into endless time.

"Pues, quiero permanecer en mi cultura, estar entre la gente que concuerde conmigo y que me respete, no por mi educación, títulos o posición social sino porque valoran mi presencia en sus vidas, valoran mi misión y porque tenemos algo en común. Respeto a las personas y sus puntos de vista y cumplo con mis obligaciones para con la sociedad en general. No guardo rencor ni odio contra nadie. Pero voy a vivir solamente una vida que al final es muy corta y quiero cumplir con mi deber antes de que yo también me vaya". *"So, I wish to stay in my culture, be among people that correspond with and respect me, not because of my education, titles, or social status, but because they appreciate my presence in their lives, appreciate my mission, and we share something in common. I don't fail in my respect towards others, their points of view, or in my obligations to society in general. I harbor no anger or bitterness towards anyone. But I have only one life to lead, one that ultimately is very short. And I too want to do what I came here to do before also leaving."*

He asked, once again piercing my eyes with his customary look, *"¿Y ya sabes qué quieres hacer de tu vida?" "You know what you plan to do with your life?"*

This time, however, I didn't shrink back as I once did as a child, *"Creo que sí papá. Esta vez, creo que sí." "Yes I do dad. This time, I believe I do."*

He responded, *"Entonces, concéntrate en lo que te hace feliz en lugar de lo que te produce tristeza o malestar. Elimina esas molestias de tu vida y deja de pensar en ellas. Vas a ver que las buenas acciones y la visión producirán una energía inagotable. La búsqueda de un destino que se basa en hacer el bien es también un proceso distinto comparado con las cosas que te producen tristeza." "Then, concentrate on those things that bring you happiness and not sadness or discomfort. Eliminate those from your life and stop thinking about them. You will see that good deeds and vision will result in boundless energy. Pursuing a destiny that is based on doing good is also a process that is distinct in comparison to those things that bring you sadness."*

It was in understanding and learning to consistently do things that result in happiness and contentment that my father and I spent long hours discussing into the night during our final days together.

2.

THE THREE REVELATIONS

Crafting comes from the imagined, the strength of the faithful,
and the blind will to act.

Little did I know 30 years ago that embracing imagination, faith, and the will to act would form the basis eventually leading to my work and creating the National Hispanic Institute. As a firm believer in imagination, my father often reminded me as a child that training my mind to imagine was a vital requirement in meeting life's challenges, responding to the opportunities that would undoubtedly be thrown my way.

Dad would often remind me, *"No dependas de los otros. Es mejor que uses tu imaginación para guiar tu vida y también para determinar tu destino." "Don't depend on others. Better to use your imagination to guide your life and also determine your destiny."*

Even today, his words remain firmly rooted in my thinking. In his view, the human ability to imagine was the most powerful way for people to break through the darkness of unfulfilled aspirations and dreams. It was this understanding of imagination that drove his and my mother's work in tough neighborhoods of Houston's Magnolia, Denver Harbor, and the Fifth Ward in the 1950s, 60s and early 70s. To them, imagination had the power to transcend race, ethnicity, culture, socioeconomics, religion, politics, age, and gender. It was also abundant and timeless to those wise enough to recognize its' endless abundance, influence, and power.

To my parents, there were no ceilings, barriers, or limits to the use of imagination. And while imagination often appeared to be endlessly large, complicated, and difficult to harness, it

15

was also the most essential ingredient that could eventually lead to important breakthroughs in reforming and refitting the social lenses that guided the young people with whom they worked.

However, my mother believed there was more than just imagination. To her, faith also represented a critical if not the most important element in attaining dreams. Many times I enjoyed listening to my parents argue whether imagination or faith was the most important. Their discussions were endless, consuming many hours on long trips to Laredo to visit relatives, or simply riding around downtown on special holidays like Christmas to look at the glittering lights in the more ex-pensive parts of town.

Having grown up in a strict Methodist home and being influenced by the work of two missionaries who helped found the El Mesias Methodist Church in Houston's Fifth Ward, Esther Nieto was deeply rooted in the belief that anything attained without a strong and continuous spiritual foundation would eventually crumble, fail, and be washed away.

My parents were the first Latino park directors in the history of the Houston Parks and Recreation. Before them the people in charge of these recreational areas were not Latinos, and the community youth felt that they were always the outsiders, the ones who only followed rules and were never the owners of their domain. Mom and Dad understood this phenomenon, remembering their life experiences as children. El Parque, or DeZavala Park, became the first Latino owned and run recreation center for the community. It was their home, where kids could practice until late in the evening, where La Ms Nieto and El Viejo Nieto made them feel invited and comfortable.

El Parque had much more significance than a place to play or hang out. It was where you went to learn about yourself, develop an identity, and celebrate who you were. The fever of ownership at the community center spread so quickly that more trophies were won by DeZavala in the late 1950s than any other center in the entire city. Back then it cost 5 cents to go to a sock hop held in a small recreation area that Mom divided by age. To keep the peace, my mother would select the community thugs to act as security. Rules were never broken. El Parque became the social center of the community, where youth could learn to get along, respect one another and enjoy winning city-wide championships.

It was through countless discussions with my parents about their work that I began forming a fun-damental understanding of how they used both imagination and faith as living, active sources of energy capable of transforming even the most resistant young people. However, El Parque was an altogether different life lesson. The park was their playground, their social laboratory to test new ideas, change thinking, and alter the behaviors of young people who daily crossed their pathways. The park was where they put their thoughts to work through sheer determination, despite the obstacles, the long draining hours, and the discouragements of nonbelievers.

In the early 1960s, I served as a first-time elementary school teacher working with emotionally disturbed and mentally retarded children. Imaginary play was my primary means of relating to these students and guiding their social development. The same approach was used a few years later in my work with young dropouts living in the same neighborhoods where I grew up. The knowledge and experience derived from my parents, who had been highly effective in their work, served as important learning opportunities in my development. Little did I realize then that years later, similar hours of silent dedication, working with few resources, and

17

being driven only by faith and imagination would place me on a 30 year journey that, at times, appeared to be little more than a vague and unrealizable dream.

When you consciously cut ties with your past, you have no alternative but to move forward despite not having a direction or understood destination. This moment came to me in an elevator after being summarily dismissed by an incoming political administration. I went from having an identity to having no identity, from having importance to not having any importance, from having name recognition to becoming a complete and total stranger. About the only thing I was able to salvage was my pride and self-respect. I learned to never look back, never grimace from rejection, and never look down on myself for the actions of others.

My mother often would remind me, *"Si quieres que las personas te respeten, primero tienes que respetarte a ti mismo. Las personas que permiten que los otros las traten mal son aquellas que se dejan usar. Nunca lo permitas, nunca permitas que te aten las manos. Defiende quién eres y exige que te respeten." "Before you want respect from others, you first have to respect yourself. A person who allows others to treat them badly is someone who lets others use him. Never let this happen, never let someone else handcuff you. Defend who you are and demand respect from others."*

Rather than allow myself to become sad or frightened by the prospect of no longer having a professional identity, I called my father to explain the situation.

"Tú tienes que abrir tu camino solo, hijo." "You have to open your own pathways, son."

His words of support continued with conviction, *"No dependas de otros. Ten fe en ti mismo y sigue adelante." "Don't rely on others. You place faith in who you are and move forward."*

Had it not been for the will that drives the human soul in those moments of personal despair, when giving up appears to be the only reasonable choice to make, the idea of the National Hispanic Institute (NHI) would not be part of our lives today.

Different in emphasis from the work of my parents, my efforts were not to curtail teenage delinquency or provide safe community recreational outlets for families. Instead my concern was in harnessing the energies, talents, and imaginative capacities of young, eager college-bound Latino high school students. My intent was to foster learning environments that would engage them in playing and experimenting with ideas to re-design, re-shape, and even re-invent the identity of the Latino community in preparation for an emerging 21st century world.

In my view, there was little purpose in remaining tied to old social perceptions that placed our value in American society at the bottom of the social ladder, made bootstrapping an enviable human quality, or continue the perception that the only way up was through knocking down barriers. I observed this phenomenon in the thinking of talented young Latinos from Austin, Texas back in the middle 1970s. Most no longer spoke Spanish and mainly hung around their white and black pals after school and on weekends. Lisa Perrigrinio, a founding member of NHI's youth in 1981, often called herself a "happy holistic Hispanic" to make a point of her lifestyle. Obviously she was kidding and, in a sense, being slightly sarcastic. But then again, as she used to say, "What do you want me to do Ernesto! Hang around with Cholos and Vatas just to prove my cultural relevancy?" Never had I seen young people so lost in their identity, culture, and sense of direction. Most felt bad that they had forgotten to speak Spanish, blaming mostly their parents for having lost their capacity to speak in their cultural tongue.

I felt that these were the youth the Latino community could least afford to lose, reject, or alienate. Something needed to be done to attract them back, get inside their thinking, and make life in the Latino community a destination in their journey and not a reason to exit. What I failed to realize was what the challenge involved. Ultimately, remaining Latino had to become more attractive and more compelling. They needed to be around other attractive, articulate, and forward looking peers. Rather than fight their impulses and mindsets as shaped by mainstream society, we focused on being Latino as the more attractive option.

An entire new generation of youth was needed to imagine, test, and construct new social realities for Latinos of the future. I needed to be part of an organized and sustained effort to radically alter beliefs and truths that caused young people to perceive themselves as racial minorities instead of being tied to a global culture of numerous countries bound together by similarities in language, culture, and histories. A shift was needed from the traditional views of seeing ourselves as rule followers to becoming rule makers. We also needed to feel comfortable with navigating dual cultural worlds while also learning to take ownership and responsibility for the quality of life we intended for ourselves. Finally, we needed to be guided by the ethical and moral standards that were rooted deeply in our heritage.

In working towards these ideals, the importance of designing community learning scenarios that were non-existent neither in high school nor in college became part of the vision. Our young future leaders needed to engage themselves in imaginary game playing that would lead them to look inwardly for answers in order to cause shifts and changes in their social perspectives and outlooks. They needed opportunities to reflect and analyze long held beliefs that would cause them to make important choices on maintaining, changing or even discarding behaviors, customs, practices, and habits no longer useful and even potentially harmful to their futures. They also needed to affirm sacred beliefs and values regarding family, religion, courage, freedom, individual rights, and the ethical treatment of others that were basic and integral to their cultural identities and place in the world.

There were no guidelines to follow or pathways to illuminate the way. The challenge was to rely mostly on imagination and faith to chart the direction. Those involved in building the NHI would have to muster the courage and will need to cast themselves into the darkness.

What was learned from these experiences has become the essence of third reality as an operating belief, concept, and metaphor. How we arrived at the answers and possibilities that eventually shaped the formation of the NHI may be interesting and, at times, worth mentioning. These historical milestones, however, are not as important as what we learned from the journey of imagining outcomes, employing faith in pursuing dreams, and having the will to act. Thirty years of constructing ideas, arguing over different options and directions, practicing the protocols of organizational development, realizing the benefits that come from collective endeavor and collaboration, and using imagination and faith as the primary means of envisioning the community we wish to form and in which we intend to live became the cornerstones that today guide our lives and the work we conduct.

In our journeys, our primary life lessons have come from compelling and exhorting ourselves to rely mostly on imagination and faith in our search for answers. The idea of not knowing and having to know in order to move forward; of wanting immediate answers and answers not being readily available; and of knowing that the solutions we most wanted had to come from our thinking instead of finding them through research drove us to consider countless possibilities in conducting the work. It also allowed us to bathe in the freedom that allows something much more important and profound to happen in our development.

In experimenting and testing different possibilities to guide our work, we were forced to eventually rely on thought that had substance and meaning, thought that made sense and was able to gain the support and involvement of the community we intended to serve. In the process of grappling for answers, selecting and testing the best alternatives possible, and finally witnessing the impact that our imagined ideas had on the lives of young people validated our efforts and fueled the imagination and faith we needed to continue. However, it was through our will to act, of putting ideas to work that finally determined whether or not there was substance and meaning to all that we had previously imagined and had invested our faith that ultimately determined the difference between imagined dreams and actual deeds.

As a young person, I had personally witnessed the work of my parents who, as children of the Great Depression, had not been afforded more than junior high educations due to the economic and racial conditions of the times. Both had suffered the loss of parents at critically young stages in their lives. Neither one of them had ever had sufficient access to the economic resources needed to gain any particular traction or advantage in life. Still they contributed so much of themselves in benefitting others. Among the many lessons I learned from watching them work with young people in the neighborhoods where we lived was that ethics, goodness, and goodwill towards others was an essential quality in building bonds with others. To them, these human qualities did not require high school diplomas, college degrees, titles, nor positions of importance.

When my father's time came at the age of 89, there were hundreds of people who crowded the chapel where his body was laid. Present were doctors, lawyers, ministers, elected public officials, relatives, longtime friends, business owners, common laborers, including former inmates who had served time in prison. When it came time to lower his body into the ground, my mother looked to me for some final words.

"Remember Santos Nieto," I said in between whispers and tears, *"as a person who gave so much to others despite life having given him so little. Imagine what we who are given much can do for those with less. All of us come equipped to change the lives of others."*

In my way of thinking, I wanted to remind those present of the amazing things people could do to change lives, despite their backgrounds, individual achievements, or educations. Some-where in my unconscious there was still resentment from the struggles Dad had to endure in his childhood, the tragedies in life he encountered, and the amount of effort he invested through his work.

If Dad were present today, he would momentarily hesitate, maybe smile a little, then forgivingly remind me that life had not been cruel to him. Instead it had provided both the challenges and the human capacities to use his imagination not only to endure, but thrive.

When my mother at 93 took her final breaths her faith was clearly evident. She softly counseled me not to be frightened in her final moments.

She reminded me as I stood uncontrollably weeping, holding her hands for the last time, *"A qué temerle, hijo, si Dios está aquí conmigo."* *"What is there to fear son, if God is here with me."*

Two fundamental beliefs were forever welded into my mind during those final moments with my parents. With Dad, I realized the importance that imagination plays in the constant human quest for answers to life's difficult and always changing challenges. From Mom, I learned that faith is a calming reassurance in making seemingly unattainable dreams come true.

The will to act comes from an internal recognition that you have nothing else to lose, nothing else to give up, nothing else to protect you except to keep moving forward, despite the odds you face. It's accepting your own physical death but never your emotional or spiritual death. The will to act comes from the silent recognition that in you is the ability to overcome and succeed no matter the price, the odds, the obstacles, the embarrassments, the put downs, and the always present prospects of ultimate failure.

Let us examine imagination, faith, and the will to act as *"los tres misterios de la vida,"* (the three mysteries of life, as Dad often described them.) In understanding these beliefs, no guidelines are intended for people to follow in order to lead happier, more relevant and productive lives. Their purpose is to share individual journeys where imagination, faith, and taking the steps to act became the driving forces that eventually led to the formation of an idea, an imagined place we now call the NHI.

Third Reality Revealed is not written to be a guideline for others to follow. Instead it is intended as a reminder of the vast, unimaginable possibilities that occur whenever we learn to rely on imagination and faith as the principle means of exploring and forming ideas that allow us to live relevant, fulfilled, and purposeful lives. The experience of Third Reality Revealed acts to free the individual from the daily routine of working eight-hour days, waiting patiently for the next promotion, reading countless articles, or watching special programs on increasing our personal development and wealth. The excitement of finding out was much more important than waiting for others to determine our futures. The idea of working for 30 years or more, waiting for retirement, and then having a special dinner to commemorate my service before going out to pasture was not my idea of pursuing relevancy and purpose.

The individuals involved in shaping the NHI were not driven by the prospect of attaining economic success, although we understood the importance of having the financial means to live in a comfortable home, being able to pay our bills, putting money away for rainy days, and working to enjoy particular lifestyles. The more compelling thought was the endless possibilities of crafting roles for ourselves that could benefit others and in the process enjoy the exhilaration that invariably comes from embracing a community so deeply rooted in our heritage and culture.

These experiences in self-learning have given me the latitude to imagine, test, and put into action concepts that the NHI community commonly refers to as third reality thinking. By shedding light on the roles that imagination, faith, and the will to act played in stirring our human spirits, we hope to play some role in making the 21st century an era where future generations of Latino leaders will look inside themselves to discover the bountiful sources of energy needed to guide community change. Future stakeholders of the Latino community must learn to rely on imaginative thinking, faith, and the courage to act as keys that unlock minds and place no barriers on the vast possibilities that can be attained by taking full command in shaping worlds they wish to create for themselves.

3.

IMAGINATION, THE FIRST REVELATION

There are no real secrets involved in understanding imagination except in accepting its existence and its powerful influence on the human mind to endlessly think creatively.

"No te rompas la cabeza para tratar de entender cosas de la vida que no tienen explicación," "Don't break your brain trying to understand things in life that have no explanation," my father often would remind me.

"Sólo acepta que la vida es así y ten confianza en ti mismo porque está esperándote allí para vivirla." "Just accept it as being there, waiting for you
to use it."

A professor friend of mine of years later often would explain culture to his students in much the same way.

"Culture," Dr. Rolando Hinjosa-Smith, English professor at the University of Texas would observe, *"is a difficult word to understand. To define culture also is to confine it. Just accept that it exists as a human phenomenon that shapes entire societies and forms their identities."*

To the curious mind, accepting imagination as simply existing without any need to explain or understand how it works may be difficult to some people. It exists, nonetheless, and is constantly in use by literally millions of people every day in their individual journeys to gain meaning and clarity. We must accept imagination as a natural part of the human experience, a gift of nature to be used in solving complex human challenges.

Imagination has been around since human beings first walked the earth. The capacity for the mind to configure never-ending forms of images, ideas, concepts, visions, perceptions, relationships, extrapolations, and so forth has been at the bottom of countless breakthroughs and the forming of new knowledge and insight throughout the history of humankind.

To me, one of the most wondrous examples of imagination is the amount of thought that undoubtedly went into the creation of three famous American documents. The Declaration of Independence established the grounds for nation-building and the principles of self-governance that eventually led to the creation of our country. The Constitution delineated the process through which our new nation would form laws to govern itself. The Bill of Rights gave each American citizen personal freedoms with the guarantee of protection against the intrusions of their own self-imagined, self-created government. Nowhere on earth, except possibly in ancient Greece, had a nation ever existed before "of and by the people."

Beyond the outrage with the despotic reign of a harshly cruel government across a giant sea, a new form of governance emerged over 200 years ago, based on perceptions, thoughts, and concepts that today fuel and illuminate how we conduct our lives. This common set of ideals, beliefs, and principles continue to serve as a model for others throughout the world to emulate. Undeniably, the formation of these three documents and eventual establishment of an entire nation did not occur out of the thin air. The collective will to imagine a way of life by a group of visionaries became the most important component in forming the beliefs and truths that created a nation. Imagination became a vital ingredient in this process, whether in reaction to a set of human challenges and conditions or the desire to lead a particular quality of life. It was in unleashing the powerful and endless influences of this energy that a new world of thinking was formed.

Many years ago after having established the National Hispanic Institute, I invited a special group of Latinos from Texas to consider serving on the board of the newly formed organization. A couple of them lived in Dallas, another two in Odessa out in West Texas. One was from Austin, two from the Texas Rio Grande Valley, and one from Houston. Each of these eight individuals, in their own right, had built successful businesses. In Houston, Phil Garza ran a trucking and transport business. Sam Moreno had a growing oil supply firm that he ran from his Dallas offices, while Pete Dominguez had built several Mexican food restaurants in the same city. Abraham Kennedy in Austin was in the Mexican food industry in Austin. Pete Diaz, Jr. owned a chain of grocery stores scattered throughout the Texas Valley, the same region of the state where Liborio Hinojosa ran his meat packing business from Mercedes. Finally, there was Willie Salinas who with his brother Mario, had built a thriving business in building oil field derricks. When attending a board meeting, they would arrive in their private planes, eager to mingle with one another, sharing advice in addressing similar challenges that transcended their business operations.

My purpose in having these Tejano millionaires on the board of directors of the NHI was not to ask them for contributions or to leverage their social capital in search of grants from government agencies. My purpose was to gain insight into the ideas that first created their individual business enterprises and the thinking that continued to make their ventures successful. From these discussions, several core lessons emerged.

The topic these individuals raised most often whenever they came together was the enormous sacrifice they had to endure in making their businesses work.

Willie and Mario Salinas from Odessa, Texas originally worked for an oil derrick welding company in Houston. Seeing that a lot of the customers came from West Texas, they decided to go at it alone. They purchased some acreage outside of Odessa and made sixteen hours their normal workday.

Abraham Kennedy and Pete Dominguez talked about getting up at three in the morning to purchase fresh fruit from area farmers' markets and, to ensure that the food was well prepared and the service was quick and efficient, stayed on top of their cooks and waiters all day and into the late evenings, six days a week. They rarely got more than four or five hours of sleep a night before they started again.

Phil Garza and his brother Ray didn't have the capital to purchase trucks, so they rented them from local dealers whenever they got contracts to move incoming containers from the hundreds of ships that daily entered the Port of Houston from all over the world. If they couldn't find enough temporary drivers to transport, it was not uncommon for them to be the principal drivers.

The same tough challenges faced other board members. Pete Diaz, Jr. drove from town to town to ensure that his chain of neighborhood convenience stores were opened on time, well managed, clean and attractive, and well stocked.

Sam Moreno faced similar challenges, traveling long distances to ensure that his growing number of oil field equipment supply stores were ready and responsive to the needs of a fiercely competitive oil industry.

Liborio Hinojosa mentioned living in the freezer sections of H&H Meat Products cutting meat all weekend in preparation for early Monday deliveries, although he was the acknowledged CEO of the business.

Each of these individuals faced enormously difficult times getting their business ventures off the ground, often facing setbacks that were seriously disheartening to their individuals visions. Yet beyond their tough dispositions, they were constantly caught up in envisioning and determining when and where they would take the next step.

Although highly successful by the time they joined the board of directors of a newly formed NHI, each had a story to tell with lessons that I would apply in my personal journey with the NHI. I learned not to expect miracles in making NHI a success. I had to be the miracle thinker and worker, not some outside force. I learned to get used to the friegas (unexpected burdens and setbacks) that invariably accompany any startup venture. I learned to accept many "Nos" before running into one "Yes" in my quest to make the organization work. I learned to be more grateful and humble instead of egotistical and self-centered whenever victories –small and large– appeared along the way. I learned to keep my nose to the grind, twenty-four hours a day, seven days a week. I learned to be prepared for the unexpected and ready to execute for sudden changes in the business. I learned to pay the salaries of others before paying myself. Mostly I learned that imagined answers were far better than those found in textbooks, and that being prepared to prove your value and worth to others would eventually become the keys to the success of the NHI.

These lessons seemed to be the operating phenomena in all of these Tejano millionaires. More than the exhilaration of watching their businesses grow, beyond the social recognition that invariably comes from attaining economic success, and in spite of the energy-draining burdens of business, these men appeared more drawn by the chase of the hunt than reaching their goals. Both were important. However, the hunger for answers, the recognition of opportunity, the cunning in their thinking, and the constant analysis of the most efficient ways of achieving their desired aims seemed to take precedence.

A common thread ran throughout in their talk. The process of the hunt and the excitement of arriving at their desired aims seemingly unleashed vast reserves of energy that propelled them towards the prize they were seeking, prepared to make adjustments through-out the chase, and helped them to rely mostly on their instincts in recognizing the precise moment to act.

I finally began to get a glimpse of imagination and its boundless possibilities, as a phenomenon that as a child my father wanted me to understand and eventually make part of my life. To him, providing young people with insight into imagination meant granting them an inheritance that would translate into valuable tools for personal goal attainment. Imagination for me became a personal freedom to seek knowledge and truths that oftentimes were elusive, beyond my capacities to comprehend. In time, learning to rely on imagination gave me the confidence and courage to pursue self-growth and self-realization. I no longer needed the assurances of a safety net in the event of failure. In the process, I learned that not having answers is neither shameful nor a reminder of darkness staring me in the face. Instead imagination became a source of personal strength, an energy that eventually allowed me to celebrate the joy that comes from the experience of having arrived at an answer through the simple act of constantly searching for new answers.

In my experience with our board of Tejano millionaires in the 1980s at the NHI, the conversation invariably turned to imagining solutions to the multiple challenges each of these individuals faced in growing and expanding their businesses. The common denominator to these discussions was that each of these persons was on a personal quest in pursuing their respective destinations. The challenge was in constantly imagining the next step, conquering the next problem thrown in their direction, being prepared for the mountain to climb. There was a certain under-standing that the nature of their efforts was more in working on their business than in their business. Each one of them appeared to have an imagined vision of the destination they were seeking. What kept them up late at night and what woke them in the early morning was that their minds never seemed to stop working, constructing new possibilities to the persistency of challenges that invariably emerged.

"Hijo, deja que tu mente vuele sin límites ni condi-ciones," "Let your mind run, without limitations or conditions, son," my Dad often would say to me during those special moments of a father and son privately chatting at the dinner table.

"La mente es un instrumento que Dios te ha dado para que puedas dirigir tu vida. Debes tener fe en tu mente para que pueda responder, para que pueda imaginar. Las ilusiones y los sueños son posibilidades que te da la mente para pensar en tus decisiones. Esto es algo que viene por naturaleza. Algo que no se aprende en las escuelas ni de los libros." "The mind is an instrument that God has given you to man-age life. Place faith on it, so it can respond and imagine. Illusions and dreams are the ways that the mind provides you with possibilities to consider in your decisions. This comes from nature, not from going to school or reading books."

Little did I realize back then that eventually the early lessons that often take place between child and parents would eventually serve to inspire the creation of the NHI. The discussions came back and interjected themselves while driving through the mountains of northern New Mexico in my search for a beginning point. Like the Tejano millionaires whom I came to know and deeply trust, I, too, had discovered an imagined quest so convincing and powerful that little time was left for anything else than the pursuit of the vision.

My father was correct. In letting the mind run free without the bias of prescriptive outcomes and goals that are external in their makeup, the search that follows always will be inward, not outward. The mind scans and gathers information that forms the makeup of the person. It gathers data on the person's history, values, beliefs, truths, likes, dislikes, tendencies, and references. The mind understands the individual's fears and apprehensions that also include the individual's aspirations, dreams, and illusions. The mind configures infinite possibilities that dwarf the traditional means through which we pursue degrees. The mind is not restrictive, punitive, callous, or rejecting. The mind presents countless options and possibilities without the external obstructions or impositions of structures, credentials or expertise that either validate or invalidate our thoughts and ideas.

As Dad would often warn me, *"Si permites que otra persona domine tus sueños o aspiraciones, si otros te hacen tener miedo, o si evades la oscuridad del no saber, entonces estás permitiendo que la inseguridad se apodere de tu libertad para imaginar. Debes tener fe en tu mente que es un instrumento muy importante en tu vida. Es fundamental que le prestes atención y que le des mucho cariño como si fuera una plantita que hay que regar constantemente para que puedas disfrutar de los beneficios que te brindará."* *"If you let another person dominate your dreams or aspirations, and if others cause you to have fear, or if you run from the darkness of not knowing, then you are allowing the insecurity of not knowing to enslave the freedom to imagine. Give it attention and love like a small plant that constantly requires water so that you may benefit from its promise."*

As normal, healthy human beings, most of us aspire to do well in life, to achieve dreams that sometimes appear beyond our reach. We equate "living the dream" with arriving at particular destinations in our lives that promise to give us a personal sense of accomplishment and contentment.

When seen through these social lenses, imagination becomes much more than a phenomenon. It also becomes a life force that plays a significant role in launching us towards the attainment of those dreams. Imagination allows the unreal to become reachable, to take on attainable possibilities. It gives us the impetus to take the first step into the unknown, to try. As a young child growing up in Houston, Saturday mornings usually were spent watching morning cartoons with my two older brothers, Albert and Roy. During commercial break, Tootsie Rolls advertised their candy in a way that left an indelible impression on me. Every time that Mickey Mantle, the famous New York Yankee baseball slugger, would step up to the plate, he would secretly reach into his pocket, take a Tootsie Roll, and causally place it in his mouth. The very next pitch could be seen being hit high, flying into the distant centerfield bleachers to the roar of cheering fans -- a Home Run!

When I was seven, while playing sandlot baseball with my neighborhood friends, I secretly reached into my pocket and pulled out a couple of Tootsie Rolls right before the next pitch. As I put in my mouth, I purposely took a second or two longer to savor the taste. At the right moment, I hit the next pitch sailing way past the outfielders as I confidently trotted around the bases, convinced that the Tootsie Rolls did the trick for me. From that moment forward, I made it point to always stop at the Midway Store to purchase several Tootsie Rolls before heading over to De Zavala Park to play ball with neighborhood friends. My frustration grew, however, because this particular brand of candy never worked again, despite trying it on several other occasions. It was then that I realized that it was mostly imagination working on my mind that momentarily made me a believer. The importance of believing in my abilities became an important life lesson that would play a large role in my work.

For me, imagination became much more than a phenomenon. It was a source of abundant energy as large as the endless universe. It also took on other forms. It became a requirement for believing, the impetus we need to risk taking the first steps into the world of uncertainty.

In my life, imagination has allowed me to overcome the paralysis of fear and the unwillingness to take the first step. It has served as a source of inspiration to take the giant leaps of faith all of us face at different points in our lives without fully knowing what to expect upon landing. It has allowed me to mentally paint different destinations in my life that represent particular meaning and have been ideas worth pursuing.

Imagination works and provides you with options when you least expect them. In my journey of nearly 31 years, imagination has been the principal means of evolving the organization, determining the next step to take, creating the next new product or ser-vice. An important difference exists between imagination and illusion, however. An illusion is something that a person thinks about far off in the distance a destination to reach, a quiet reprieve from the daily hustle and bustle of life. Taking off to the beach for the weekend fulfills the illusion of kicking back and relaxing, being with friends, getting off the fast moving train of life for a moment to pause and take a breath of fresh air. Illusions disconnect a person from realities. Not so with imagination. Imagination energizes a per-son to think and perceive in fast-forward, to investigate, and to form and test new possibilities in the brain before committing them to paper or action. Imagination works constantly in a per-son, never sleeping, like a computer that remains working long after the person goes to sleep.

Many times, I have gone to bed purposely thinking of a challenge in order to let my brain work on it as I sleep. And often, I've gotten up in the middle of the night with several possibilities that at that precise moment either have to be entered into my computer or face the possibility of forever fading beyond recovery. I've come to the conclusion that a person can train the brain to imagine, letting it loose without direction, other than total latitude to construct, perceive, sense, and invent possibilities that go beyond what the conscious mind is able to handle.

Imagination, without being activated, becomes a senseless vacuum, a means of losing important time. When used correctly, imagination can be activated to work twenty-four hours a day. While the rest of the world sleeps, imagination quietly is at work like an artist captured in a world of silence constantly inventing, testing, scanning, and evaluating. At times it becomes the alarm clock that awakens oneself in the early morning hours, excited about a new thought, a new possibility, a breakthrough that has to be consciously explored or written down in a reminder note. Imagination is a preview of ideas and concepts in the creative state, anxiously awaiting their moment to be discovered.

4.

FAITH THE SECOND REVELATION

Faith is a protection from the unknown,
a shield against the weakness of the human spirit.

Whether faith comes before imagination is like trying to determine whether the egg came before the chicken or vice versa. What is known is that faith is as vital as oxygen is to life. It represents one of three mysteries of life, as my father called them.

A friend of many years, a school superintendent whose daughter and son participated in the Institute's Lorenzo de Zavala Youth Legislative Session, spent considerable time trying to understand what drove NHI's work. One evening over dinner, he leaned back and said, *"After really thinking about what keeps the Institute growing and expanding, I've determined that it isn't the availability of funding, following a strategic plan, or having a large staff to assist you with your efforts. While having access to these resources are important to any organizational effort, they really haven't played that much of a role in your work."*

Dr. Roberto Rodriguez paused for a moment, leaned back on his chair and then said, "The NHI operates under the POOF Theory."

"You see," he went on, *"I've seen that whenever you can't figure out whether to go in this direction or that one; or whenever you decide to do something different and challenging, you turn and look around for a second or two and then snap your fingers and holler 'POOF' almost like a Genie working her magic."*

Robert leaned over and said, *"So I've taken the expression you so commonly use along with snapping your fingers and call it the POOF THEORY, meaning Proceed Only on Faith."* POOF!

My friend was close to the truth as I learned to see it. I became accustomed to hollering out "Poof!" whenever I was caught in a dilemma with no apparent answers or directions to follow. First talks were held among staff about the various alternatives open to us and the consequences and rewards associated with each possible choice. Eventually we would end up having to select from one of several possibilities and would almost always conclude with saying "Poof!" and then snapping our fingers as though magically arriving at a conclusion. Once a choice was made, the idea was to make our decisions work for us, proceeding only on faith.

One of my first encounters with faith came as an eight-year-old youngster back in my old neighborhood of Magnolia in Houston. On the corner of Avenue H where we lived stood an empty, old two-story house that had been abandoned for as long as we had lived there. The front door remained slightly open most of the time, but never enough to where anything inside could be seen. There were no lights on inside or on the first or second story porches. The window screens were old, rusty, and at times torn as though someone had either tried to get in or suddenly get out. The back part of the house had paint peeling off the exterior walls and a screen door that could be heard flopping against the frame entrance on windy evenings. Making the house even scarier was an old leaning picket fence that surrounded the house along with overgrown weeds, broken bottles, and old cans scattered about. All of us as young boys instinctively knew to stay away from this place. Rumors flew around the older neighborhood kids that in the past, younger children who had been seen entering this place had never been seen again.

To Pacho, Mingo, and Israel, the brothers who lived across the street, as well as me and my two brothers, this was not a place to go play during the day or at night. Our imaginations were especially stirred on late evenings when the house stood mysteriously silent, silhouetted against a radiant October night moon and slightly hidden behind the subtle movement of darkened clouds.

One cool Saturday evening after listening to Dad's scary stories about dogs with rabies in Laredo, Texas, while huddled together sitting on the front porch of our home, all five of us quietly decided to demonstrate our lack of concern for the dark by daring each other to individually walk through the downstairs and upstairs of the abandoned two story house. Only one person was permitted to go at a time. By then, Albert was eleven years old, the oldest of the group. He was followed by Roy, my middle brother and then Israel. Afterwards came Mingo at nine years old and finally Pacho and I at eight. The rules were that none of us would do anything out loud that would startle our parents into coming inside the house. By then it was almost eleven at night and Mom and Dad were starting to get ready for bed and church the next morning.

Albert was the first to go, silently disappearing into the house, taking what seemed an eternity and then running back across the street where we were anxiously waiting, huddled together underneath a large tree on the front lawn of our house. Roy followed afterwards. Then came Israel and Mingo. Each one of then returned with their own accounts of what they either saw or imagined was there. Pacho revealed an instance on the second floor where he could clearly hear something breathing inside a closed closet door, but was too afraid to suddenly open it for fear of what was lurking in the dark. All five of them turned to me as though communicating the unsaid, the final dare.

"You have to open the closed door on the second floor to see what's inside," came the command of my oldest brother, Albert as he momentarily stared at me. This was not the time to show fear or demonstrate any need to seek the protection of parents. Besides, all my classmates at De Zavala Elementary would know the very next day that I was a scaredy-cat when confronted with the challenge. The Tamayo brothers, though being our best friends and neighbors across the street, would love nothing better than spread the news that the Nieto's were "chicken." This couldn't happen, no matter the fear of the consequences stirring in my head or boiling inside the stomach of a frightened and desperate eight year old. All it took was the final look on the eyes of my two older brothers not to let them down that silently nudged me in the direction of the house, not knowing whether to scream out loud or suddenly run inside the safety of my home to the waiting and comforting arms of Mom.

Each step that brought me closer to the half opened door made the house appear gigantic, powerful, threatening.

Mom's reassuring words suddenly gushed inside my mind. *"Ten fe en Dios. Sólo debes decir: yo tengo fe," "Just say, I have faith. You put your faith in God,"* She would often counsel us, especially me as her youngest.

"Cuando te sientas sólo, busca a Dios en tu cora-zón. Ya verás que en la oscuridad de la vida, Dios será tu luz y te protegerá." "When finding yourself alone, look for God in your heart. In the darkness of life, God is your light and God will protect you, you'll see."

With each step I took towards the awaiting evil lurking inside the house, I kept repeating through my gritted teeth, "I have faith, I have faith." The entire time my hands were clenched, my eyes and ears anxiously alert to anything strange, each step bring-ing me closer to the front door. Suddenly, almost without notice, I stepped inside. Having taken this giant leap of faith, however, was only the beginning. There was an entire darkened house to walk through, including the closed closet door where sounds had been heard earlier. I nervously scanned the inside and began curiously exploring the downstairs room by room to the creaking sounds of old boards, torn wall paper hanging form the ceilings, the sound of field mice hiding under the kitchen cabinets by the sink, and spider webs stretching across door entrances. Finally came the upstairs to the bedrooms and the dreaded hall closet!

Over and over, I repeatedly kept whispering, *"I have faith, I have faith,"* poised at any moment to come face to face with the ugliest, scariest, most vile monster any boy at eight years of age could conjure in his mind. With eyes wide open and frozen face ready to look directly in the face of the unknown, I suddenly and with every breath in my trembling body screamed as loud as I could, *"I have faith!"* I suddenly reached to grab the handle of the door and swung it open, ready to confront my fate and ultimate death.

The entire neighborhood must have heard my gut wrenching scream as a few porch lights came on with people looking through the cracks of their front doors, curiously trying to find out what had just happened. Mom also came out on the front porch quickly looking over to where my friends and brothers were standing, realizing that I was missing.

"¿Dónde está Ernesto?" she asked sternly in a manner that only boys understand when moms question them in a certain way. Almost in a choreographed response they timidly turned towards the house where I stood exhausted, standing outside on the front porch. I weakly made my way across the street towards her as she quietly took my hand and gently led me inside our home.

"Ya acuéstense muchachos. Ya es tarde y mañana tenemos que ir a la iglesia." "Go to sleep now. It's late and tomorrow we have to go to church."

No other words were needed.

In my life trajectory, faith has undoubtedly played a huge role. Faith in my world has played multiple roles and comes in many forms. When making the decision to no longer look back on a former life or spend time doubting whether or not to proceed forward in establishing the Institute, faith became the force that propelled me forward. When angrily shouting at the darkened skies in Houston after my brother Albert, the last surviving member of the family in which I was born into took his last and final breath, it was faith in a greater design that tenderly brought me back to my senses.

Mother used to remind me as a young boy,

"Un día de estos, te vas a encontrar solo, triste y confundido en el mundo. Pero no tienes nada que temer. Ponte de pie y ten fe en Dios. Él te dará consuelo y refugio." "One day, you will find yourself alone in the word, confused and saddened. There is no need for you to fear. Get on your knees and place your faith in God. He will give you comfort and refuge."

My mother never told me that faith would ever help me work out my problems or ease my concerns. She only reminded me that faith would stand by me through my darkest hours or give me the courage to act when facing the unknown. It was in the demonstration of faith where she would invariably make her point in ways remarkably different from my father.

Mom rarely spoke whenever my father was counseling or correcting us as three young boys. She would sit down at the kitchen table with Dad and me, always reading her newspaper, silently moving her lips to catch every printed word. Reading was her passion. Only on rare occasions would she interrupt. All of us, however, knew that when she spoke, our job was to listen. Even the enthusiasm of a father caught up in teaching us about life would be momentarily silenced, often taken back by the depth of her counsel.

"Dios es muy grande y poderoso, hijo. En su plan, sólo somos un puñado de arena. Sé humilde ante su presencia y Él te dará infinita sabiduría. Él será la luz que te guiará cuando pases por momentos oscuros. Pero todo esfuerzo requiere dedicación y no debes dejar que tus amiguitos te lleven de aquí para allá. Analiza todo y después concéntrate en tus metas." "God is powerful and all encompassing, son. In his plan, we are but grains of sand. Humble yourself in his presence and he will give you endless know-ledge. He will be your guiding light in your moments of darkness. But effort also requires dedication and not letting your little friends pull this way and that way. Study everything and then dedicate total attention to your goals."

Even today in my older years, I still quietly slip away into a small bedroom at home, and quietly kneel by an old chair from our original El Mesias Methodist Church in Houston's Fifth Ward. Years ago, my mother had taken this artifact from the church's back room where old discarded furniture was piled up and forgotten. She had it restored to its original look. My grandmother Emilia Alfaro once had it in her home and now, many years later, it sits in mine, almost a century later.

Whenever I am in doubt or concerned about life's many challenges, I go to the room where Mom once slept when she visited me. There I kneel down and begin praying. Almost always, I get back up feeling refreshed, certainly strengthened in my faith, and reassured that both my mother and father would be very approving in ob-serving their youngest son put into practice what they once taught him.

Faith has undoubtedly been a main fixture in the work of NHI. It was faith that originally led me to dedicate my life to the work, knowing fully well that there was no money and no prospects of anyone helping except in learning to first help myself. It was faith that repeatedly brought me back to continue the mission when doubt or the forces of opposition became too great to bear. It was also faith that propelled me to continue when faced with personal tragedies in my life, the loss of my father, followed by my mother and immediately afterwards, my last remaining brother, Albert, "Uncle Louie."

Faith became that remarkable, inexplicable mystery that saw me through many moments of confusion, darkness, and incoherence. Like imagination, I came to appreciate and value faith as existing in enormous and endless amounts.

Faith, however, is much more profound. Without it, imagination has no direction or purpose. Faith exists as a phenomenon and force that is endless. It impacts our every day lives. And depending on how the person chooses to harness and channel it, faith can become the armament that not only shield us against the frailties of feeling unprotected and vulnerable in life as human beings, but also fuels our self dignity and self respect when con-fronted with our very end. In this context, faith allows us to leap out and free ourselves from our physical presence on earth to join others in a journey into time and space that has no limit or end.

5.

WILL TO ACT THE THIRD REVELATION

The will to act arms us with the courage to enter the wilderness of life, determined to survive the unexpected.

The will to act and the human drive to endure are essentially one in the same. Some call this drive overcoming adversity or remaining focused on the outcome. In training his players, Guy Lewis, legendary basketball coach at the University of Houston, used to make reference to "intestinal fortitude," or paying the price of success. In other words, there must be a conscious recognition of an outcome far superior and attractive than the requirements of preparation in order to strive towards a particular life goal or vision. This conscious recognition keeps the person on task, focused on the goal, and committed to the step-by-step process often associated in getting to a desired outcome.

Through the years, I've come to believe that our unwillingness to act on our ideas is all too often stifled by the fear of failure or inability to forecast the outcome. A longtime friend, Rudy Flores, who was special assistant to the late Governor of Texas, Dolph Briscoe, would often observe that one of the problems of Latinos having a college education was the tendency to over-analyze all of the things that could possibly go wrong whenever faced with the prospect of pursuing an important idea or business venture.

Rudy would lean back on his office chair laughingly and say, *"Una persona pobre y sin educación que no entiende las consecuencias, casi nunca piensa en los problemas que se podrían presentar cuando trata de iniciar un negocio. Para aquél que empieza sin nada, no tiene nada que perder o que puedan quitarle. No tiene ningún título que perder.*

Todo lo que hace en la vida es el resultado de la desesperación, no para proteger sus intereses. Es por eso que el Latino que es dueño de un negocio en muchos casos no es muy educado. Al contrario, es el educado quien más teme a las consecuencias y al final, prefiere poner excusas por hacer poco." "A poor, uneducated person doesn't understand consequences, he rarely spends time thinking about problems that can possibly occur whenever trying to respond to establish a business. For a person who begins with nothing, there is nothing to lose or be taken away. There is no title to lose. Whatever they do comes out of desperation in life, not to protect their interests. That's why the Latino who owns a business in many cases doesn't have a lot of education. To the contrary, is the one with the education that most fears the consequences and in the end prefers to make excuses for doing little."*

I really had not spent too much thought on what Rudy had shared with me until a few years later, after being suddenly dismissed from my job by an incoming political administration in state govern-ment that wanted to select its own top officials. From one moment to another, I was called into a side office and asked to clear out my desk in the next 20 minutes. Within moments, I went from being Ernesto Nieto, executive assistant at the Texas Department of Community Affairs, an office of the Governor, to Ernesto Nieto, nothing.

Beyond the sudden shock of having worked most of my life to land a top policy role in govern-ment only to be summarily dismissed without notice or cause, other feelings and thoughts slowly crept into my psyche. For a moment, I felt like a young puppy being dumped off on some lonely highway far out in the distant woods with nowhere to turn or go, except to sheepishly look about in unfamiliar surroundings not knowing which direction to take. Being in the midst of divorce proceedings only added to an inner feeling of quiet desperation, knowing that I had four young children to feed and bills to pay.

Rudy had been right in his earlier observations. What else was there to lose? Certainly not my title or professional reputation. These had already been abruptly removed. I was sharing a small apartment with an old friend waiting for my divorce papers to be finalized and had no money left at the end of the month after paying child support. Having my children enjoy the stability and comfort of having a home was much more important during these trying moments than my personal living needs. In the process of this experience, there was no one running to me with business offers or new job possibilities.

Ben McDonald, former Mayor of Corpus Christi, put it best when discussing the raw truth about politics: "there are moments in one's life that you can call all your friends with a quarter." This was me, January, 1979.

Rudy popped into my thinking one more time. There was nothing else for me to lose. One option was to continue looking for a job to meet the daily needs of my family, fully aware of what to expect in the end. My second choice was entering into the realm of the unpredictable, the unexpected, in my attempts to derive a sense of purposeful meaning and relevance in my life endeavors.

People often find themselves at these particular crossroads in their individual life journeys. Most spend long hours peering into the darkness, not knowing which direction to take, first weighing all the possible options before considering the next step to take. Depending on their circumstances, most look backward instead of forward. They repeatedly recount and analyze all of the events and instances that brought them to particular points in their lives. Sometimes they become angry or even disappointed at not recognizing and acting at precise moments to counteract the directions that life took them. In seek-ing solutions to their dilemmas, however, most rarely take the next step forward, electing instead the safer grounds of predictability, promising themselves not to repeat the same mistakes again, but doing little to change their perspectives, outlooks and mental models they continue using in navigating their lives.

Having the will to act and making a deter-mined effort to take a new and bold step into the unknown requires more than courage. For many of us, venturing into uncharted waters is driven by the realization that certain outcomes are guaranteed to occur if we remain anchored to the same beliefs and truths that have always driven us.

People of great accomplishments have not been spared these discouraging experiences in their daily lives. Most all of them have faced similar circumstances, including financial loss, business failures, death of loved ones in their families, illness, and other serious setbacks. These challenges may erode the human spirit and draw into question whether the pursuit of particular life goals are worth the effort, yet for successful individuals the outcomes were remarkably similar.

For most, finding the will to continue becomes the court of last resort when imagination dims their vision and their faith is questioned. During these momentous points in their lives, will protects them against the temptations of either looking at the prospects of failure or turning back. Will becomes the prime source of strength to continue moving forward, the one element that awakens them in the middle of the morning and compels them to get up and keep moving.

The work of the Institute extends far beyond the notions of individual effort. No doubt that many people see me as the titular head of the organization as its founder and current president. The work, however, and my preparation for it began years before. Having this sense of history, background, and shared purpose with my parents and brothers is the driving energy that personally provides me with the faith and vision to continue ahead no matter the obstacles or discouragements that invariably appear along the pathways of life.

Dad stood right next to my side in front of the Victorian Mansion when we first purchased it and said, "Nunca pierdas este lugar, hijo. Protégelo para que pueda inspirar a aquellos que creen en esta misión y en el trabajo." "Never lose this place. Protect it so that it may inspire those who believe in this mission and the work."

Mom loved the old place because it reminded her of the days when people sat on porches looking out, sharing lemonades and cookies casually discuss-ing life.

Behind the mansion is a special cluster of five Texas Live oak trees that I selected one day in memory of my family. A wrought iron face built by a local welder and personal friend distinguishes this small modest plot from the other trees. Two of the Texas oaks are woven together, as my parents were when they first married and remained husband and wife for sixty-three years. I never saw two people love each other more in my entire life. The other remaining three trees are symbols of my brothers Roy, Albert, and I, as the youngest. All of my original family members are gone now except for me. I suppose I'm the last soldier standing.

During moments of personal despair, con-fusion, special remembrance or even celebration, I quietly go there to think and reflect. During those instances, the world stops for several moments, and I sometimes quietly kneel down to touch the rose bush that I planted for Mom. I imagine Mom's quick wit and laughter at the craziness of life, always reminding me to be thankful and never steer away from my values and deep belief in God. I think about Pop's amazing philosophy of life and the practicality with which he approached difficulties along his journey. To him, every challenge, every problem had a solution but only for those willing to dedicate their time to deep thought and study. Roy was Mr. Charisma, the guy with the contagious smile, the person who would have certainly been the millionaire of the family. Albert, as I came to realize many years later, was a special angel in my life who admired me deeply and was so thrilled to know that he had done something special for someone else.

In my moments of craziness at times, while standing at this special place at the NHI, I gaze up at the stars and imagine myself having a conversation with all of them at once. I envision us sitting around the table with our heads bowed praying for forgiveness and always thanking God for having given us such joys in life. Someday soon, I will become the fifth tree in the small clump of Texas oaks and like the other trees; I will become a fading memory of a life and cause that once was. Until that moment comes, I will continue to be energized and driven by the conscious recognition of being part of a family tradition and vision much larger than me and much larger than my family.

As Dad invariably would remind me, "Hijo, al final del día, no se trata de lo que acumulaste en dinero, títulos o prestigio en la vida, sino en el uso que le diste a las cosas que te dieron para beneficiar al mundo mientras estuviste aquí. Hay tres cosas que son seguras: todos, el pobre, el rico y el que comete crímenes, tienen el mismo fin. Nuestros días en este mundo se terminan y todos nos convertimos en polvo. ¡Recuerda! Aprovecha bien tu tiempo mientras estés aquí." "Son, at the end of the day, it's not what you accumulate in money, titles or prestige we have in life, but instead what we do with what was given to us to benefit the world. Three things are certain. The poor man, the rich one, and the criminal all reach the same end. Our time on earth ends and we all turn to dust. Remember! Use your time well while you're here."

When proceeding forward in the work of NHI, our conversations were endless when imagining all the possibilities that could take place. What really mattered was having the faith that we were correct in our hearts and that our intentions were good ones. The time came, however, when the decision to continue the journey was up or down, red light or green light, no more cautions. There was no more reconsideration, no more last minute reasons to pull back, pause, or hesitate.

Essentially broke at our inception, the NHI occupied a couple of small offices in an abandoned annex building where Concordia University used to store old furniture. The staff consisted of mostly volunteers, a part-time hourly person, and myself. Arriving by seven, and certainly no later than eight in the morning, was customary for everyone. Working until midnight, at times sleeping on the floor because it was too late to return home just to get back up and start working again was more customary than not. Back then, there were no computers, no call forward-ing services, and little in modern technology to ease the load.

Many times, in pitch darkness at three or four in the morning while lying in bed pretending to be asleep, the thought of potential failure would repeat-edly rear its ugly head. During those particular moments, will becomes the only source of strength to continue moving forward. I no longer expected good things to happen. I prepared for the worst, and was willing to accept whatever consequences were lurking in the darkness of failing to reach our destination.

At times there was humor involved in facing the possibilities of failure. As a child, I didn't come from wealth or having access to people of power and influence. I was nothing more than a naïve individual who originated as a kid from the barrios of Houston and had these grand notions and designs about doing something significant with my life in the Latino community. That was it, nothing more!

In my attempts to gain a more insightful understanding of will, I've come to see it as a phenomenon that constantly interfaces with our lives during different intervals in our individual journeys through time and space. Like imagination and faith, will constitutes the third revelation in understanding how we self-construct new realities. To define will is to enter a useless endeavor. Accepting its presence is more practical, as an endless source of energy that exists in each one of us as part of our heritage as human beings, ready to be marshaled in our darkest moments of despair and when approaching barriers that appear to difficult to cross.

Sam Moreno, a father-like figure and longtime mentor of mine, faced some of the darkest moments any human being could bear experiencing. After having lost a son who died at young age from an undiagnosed heart infection, he had to face the demise of a highly successful business that he had spent the majority of his life building. Despite these life tragedies and monumental setbacks that would stop most people dead in their tracks, his will to overcome transformed him into a remarkable individual to whom others look to for counsel and guidance in trying times.

One of these moments came after the death of my last remaining brother Albert in 2003. Several weeks after the burial, I gathered enough courage to call Sam Moreno, a life-long mentor who was 15 years older. My purpose was simple. I wanted to hear his comforting words. Sam and I became friends in the 1970s while living in Dallas. Belonging to the same church, he stood next to me during some of my more trying days of going through severe panic attacks as a young 30 year old professional. This time the call came 32 years later.

"Hey Sam," I started. "Just called you to talk a little." Sam already knew about Albert. His response was as startling then as it continues to be today.

"It doesn't ever stop," he responded, "does it?"

"What do you mean Sam?" I replied, confused about the direction of our conversation.

"Life," he said laughingly, "it just keeps on throwing challenge after challenge at us, doesn't it?"

"Look Ernesto," he continued, "I know about your brother and really feel for you. I understand the pain, believe me. I've gone down that pathway several times in my lifetime and it doesn't get any better. But look at this way, what does this mean for you? Do you stand up? Do you dwell endlessly on what just happened in your life? You see, life continuously throws bullets at people and one of those bullets has your name on it. So you may be next, maybe one of your children, a really close friend, who knows. During those moments, you have to get up, take whatever memories and lessons you gained from your loving brother and move on."

"The only reserve you can rely on has little to do with your job, title, or what you do with your time. That reserve is called will the blind determination to continue on your life quest in a manner that gives you a personal sense of purpose and destination. Will is the only thing that will ultimately help you, along with the memories and assurances that your brother loved, and continues to love you deeply."

My father used to say something similar, *"No llores por aquellos que ya no están en este mundo, hijo. Ellos ya descansan y están en un lugar mejor. Llora por nosotros, los que nos quedamos aquí sólo con el sufrimiento de los recuerdos de aquellos que estuvieron en nuestras vidas."* *"Don't cry for the ones whose lives have ended on this earth, son.*

They are resting and find themselves in a better life. Cry for us who are left behind here suffering from only being left with memories of who these individuals were in our lives."

In this context, will became the third revelation for change. It is the blind determination to prevail, to keep moving forward, no matter the odds, the obstacles, the endurance required, or the enormity of the task involved.

You quietly go about the task of doing what is required without consideration for personal comforts, the exhausting long hours, and the looming possibilities of failure. You rely mostly on focus, looking only at the goal, never considering retreat or defeat, with only the reassuring knowledge that you have what it takes to get there, no matter what.

Through all of the distractions, detours, dead-ends, and even moments when life suddenly stops such as death of a loved one, the end-journey remains unchanged. It is not ego, either, that keeps the heart pounding, the energy flow going, the dream alive. Long ago, I convinced myself that establishing an Institute for Latinos in the United States was indeed something worth pursuing, a venture demanding a lifetime of dedication. Admittedly at times, the pathways along the way have been as undefined and murky as the vision itself. The outcome hasn't always been clear, but instead vague and at times difficult to see through the confusing and distracting influences of life. There have also been moments when the very idea and concept of an Institute for Latinos has been severely questioned, maybe even mocked as unreal or unrealizable. During the lonely moments of self-doubt, confusion, and loss of continuity, the person is left with little except to continue moving forward without any knowledge of the outcome or expectation of what the road ahead has to offer. In this context, the will to act becomes a moment to pause, refuel, adjust the social lenses, and reaffirm the quiet confidence of knowing that the only person who ultimately has to believe in your dream is you.

Realizing that your ideas work and are benefitting others is far richer to self-worth and extends beyond the rewards that any person could possibly imagine. The look in the eyes of a young person who thanks you for being part of a life changing experience represent a form of gratitude that is more humbling than exhilarating. Witnessing nearly 1,200 volunteers who yearly participate in the Institute's leadership learning experiences underscores the realization that young people gain much more from giving than receiving. By far the most important realization is in being both a partner and a witness to an organization that started out with only a small dream in 1979 and today has young people who annually participate from as many as 22 states and eight Latin American countries 31 years later.

Will is an undefined human force that keeps the person going even when all of the other dash board indicators of our lives are lit up, telling us to abandoned ship, to stop what we're doing. It's in all of us and in abundant amounts. It drives us to work extra hard at night when everyone else has gone to bed. It shields us against criticism when others are forecasting our failure. It reinforces our determination to succeed, to continue looking for answers when none seem apparent, to let repeated failure roll off our shoulders knowing that an answer is right ahead.

Will is much more than sheer energy. It fuels the mind to keep going forward, to take the extra step, make a last ditch effort, and remain awake late at night assessing new possibilities, new approaches to get to a particular destination or life goal. Will accepts the prospects of failure and the possibilities of falling short.

The difference between will, faith, and imagination is best described in what my father would often tell me, "La voluntad de actuar de acuerdo con nuestros deseos no sólo depende de nuestra fe e imaginación. La voluntad surge cuando ignoramos los obstáculos y la gente que nos desanima. Es necesario que te concentres completamente en tus metas y que no permitas que nada ni nadie se interponga en lo que deseas alcanzar. Lo más importante que debes asegurar es la certeza de tu visión que será tu fuente de inspiración. Esto te dará todas las fuerzas necesarias para enfrentar cualquier obstáculo." "The will to act on our ambitions doesn't only depend on imagination and faith. Will comes from being blind to obstacles as well as those who discourage you. It requires that you main-tain complete concentration on your goals and not let anything or anyone get in the way of what you wish to achieve. The most important thing for you to assure yourself is the certainty of your vision, that which inspires you. This is what gives you the strength required so that you may overcome whatever obstacles you have to confront."

6.

CHALLENGES OF COURAGE

Calling on the universal powers of imagination, faith,
and the will to act is the first step in crafting the new.

The process of internal change begins the moment you develop the courage to take a close, hard look at yourself. For me it began when I was dismissed from my executive level job in state government. You feel like everything about you is exposed for everyone to see and judge. The thought that repeatedly took place in my mind was that someone else could dictate my future, determine whether or not I ate or could provide for my children, and alter the lifestyle and dictions I took. The feeling was one of complete vulnerability and personal embarrassment. At the time, it didn't appear to me that life could ever get worse. Little did I know that after taking a closer and deeper look into myself, internal change would become be such a feared and yet liberating experience. Confession is an important first step, learning to vomit out what keeps your in-sides uncomfortable.

Visiting my parents to share the dismissal from my job, after driving from Austin to Houston in the middle of the night with my children asleep in the back seat, was my first encounter with this form of change. Collecting myself and learning to stand up straight came from kicking rocks around the mountain trail ways of northern New Mexico and rides on long dusty highways of West Texas. Reflection, anger, despair, along with feeling abandoned, alone, and without purpose were all part of the self-assessment process. Most of my beliefs came under scrutiny. What happened to fairness or the opportunity to defend myself? What happened to my friends? Why didn't anyone defend or come to my aid? Why was I left alone when I most needed support? What led me to believe that anyone cared in the first place?

This beginning self-inquiry eventually led to deeper questions. Operating beliefs and views that I had long held to be true about my identity and work came under my own intense criticism. Was I really there to serve others or was the title I had come to hold more important? Had my role in government been more about power brokering and being important in the eyes of friends and associates, or did I enjoy having a role in changing lives in the community that I talked about serving? The answers that came to mind were at first not complimentary to my self-image. To the contrary, a different view of myself began to emerge, one that made me feel self-centered, even narcissistic. Yet the process was needed if I was going to eventually understand my calling or consider pursuing a different life direction.

No doubt that cleansing the mind and de-cluttering thinking are vital first steps in changing from within. At a given time, a particular realization emerges, much like the time that I sat up after expelling my grief at the site of my brother Roy's grave. All the crying, all the kicking and screaming, all of the anger and human desperation was not going to bring him back. One is left alone to look around wondering what to do next, to sit back up again, and continue moving forward. Internal turmoil comes after confession, extreme internal conflict, acceptance, and finally the will to stand up again and continue moving forward. Only those willing to endure the disconnect, the incoherence that follows the crushing blows of altering realities ever learn to redefine their truths, and in doing so, construct a new landscape and pathways leading into the future.

When fueled by imagination, faith, and the will to act, there are no barriers strong enough to dis-courage the human spirit to succeed. Nothing may limit the individual from searching for new options and alternatives to attain particular aims and goals, or heighten the possibilities of personal failure. Failure is never the end-result of not meeting a goal or mission. Failure is the decision to no longer act when one is confronted by the obstacles that in-variably emerge in attempting to attain important life goals or reach imagined outcomes.

It was my mother who always encouraged me to learn from my mistakes and failures as a child, *"La vida, hijo, sirve de maestro. Cuando fracases o falles en algo, no te fijes en el resultado sino en lo que aprendiste con tus acciones y decisiones. La vida ofrece oportunidades que favorecerán tu preparación y aumentarán tus capacidades." "Life, son, serves as a personal teacher. Each setback, every time you fail at something, never fix your vision on the outcome, but instead the lesson you gained from your actions and decisions. From life comes the oppor-tunities to further your preparation and broaden your capacities."*

She would often remind me, even as a young adult, *"La fe nunca puede faltar en tu vida, en los caminos que recorras, cuando uses tu imaginación y cuando tomes decisiones." "Faith is what can never fail you in life at whatever roads in life you find yourself, the use of your imagination, and acting on your decisions."*

It wouldn't be until many years later that these lessons would begin to take on real life meaning and applications. Too much of my life had been spent following blueprints, buying books on personal development, searching for short cuts to my professional goals, concentrating on all the right things that ultimately would lead to individual success. Graduating from high school, getting a college degree from a respected institution, and even pursuing advanced studies were all part of this formula. So were meeting the right people, wearing the appropriate clothes, having the social skills, being seen at the right places, and having the money to go places. In my thinking, all I needed was patience in order to wait for the right moment to be discovered. Rarely did I stop to ask myself the questions of where I was going, for what reasons, what ultimate gains did I expected to achieve, and on what faith?

One day during a period of personal reflection, I came to answer some of these questions. By then my life had reached several disillusionments and setbacks. Emotionally and psychologically, most everything had inwardly become darkened by disappointment and failure. I stood in stark contrast to an exterior that often reflected strong self-confidence and boldness.

What my mother failed to prepare me for probably on purpose was that life's lessons are highly self-revealing and do not hide or soften the truth. The stark realization of making my need for personal title, power and recognition, and self-importance my prime motivation and drive in life became a disheartening revelation of my personal makeup. No confessions were required or the need to seek counsel from others. Confronting my life for the very first time gave me valuable insight into my journey. It allowed me to realize the consequences that came from the behaviors, attitudes, and outlooks that framed my views of life and relationships with others. Finally, confronting my own beliefs led me to accept full responsibility for my actions without blaming other individuals or my own life circum-stances, tragedies, or setbacks. This self-confrontation became the first step in my transformation and initial experience in the concept of third reality.

Internal change causes a person to struggle and sometimes to come into conflict with previously held personal beliefs and truths. Most of these internal references take years to construct, and are generally not subject to immediate change. They form a framework that people use to carefully weigh and evaluate their actions and express support or opposition to ideas under consideration. Some of these views and attitudes are inherited as children from parents and other significant persons in our lives. Others are influenced from our individual life experiences or imported by people we consider as being important and in the know. And then there are the beliefs and outlooks that we incorporate into our social outlooks as a result of information we read, research we conduct, or life encounters we experience.

Some beliefs are stronger and more embedded in our psyches than others. For me, internal change went to the core of my identity, the essence of my being. Everything was put on the table for close scrutiny and examination, from my religious and political outlooks to my perceived identity and place in the world. Was being Latino a vitally important aspect of my identity? Could I be everything to everyone in my journey through life? Where did I feel most comfortable, embraced, and valued? In what situations did I feel most distant, alienated, and disconnected? These were only some of the many questions that took residence in my mind for weeks and even months in my attempts to clarify and re-focus my life. My most difficult question to answer was not only deciding who I was, who I had allowed myself to become, and who I wished to become, but also how I planned to arrive at my imagined destination.

As my mother would whisper to me at night as a young boy, *"No le tengas miedo a la verdad, hijo. Porque en la verdad encontrarás tu liberación, las soluciones que calmarán tus angustias y la luz que iluminará tus caminos. Pero primero, debes tener fe en el todopoderoso. Ponte de pie y pídele que te perdone y que te guíe. De ahí vienen la imaginación y la inspiración que necesitas para alcanzar tus metas. Al final, solamente tú puedes dar tus primeros pasos hacia tu destino. Esto no viene de otros, sólo de ti."* *"Don't fear the truth, son. Because from truth comes self-liberation, the solutions that ease your anxieties and the light that illuminates your pathways in life. But first, have faith in the almighty and powerful. Get on your knees and ask for forgiveness and direc-tion. From that comes imagination and the in-spiration required to reach your goals. In the end, only you can take the first steps towards your des-tination. That doesn't come from others; it only comes from you".*

These lessons taught me to first work on learning to change myself before attempting to change the lives of others. They gave me a framework to look critically at my strengths and weaknesses, and forecast potential threats, so that I could begin taking steps to correct my life directions. Other lessons would come from counsel that became time-less in their teachings.

To Esther Nieto, a disciplined mind was the core ingredient to remain focused in reaching important life goals.

"No le prestes atención a tus amiguitos cuando se rían de ti o te critiquen. Tranquilamente, sepárate de ellos para concentrarte en tus sueños. Un día de estos, ellos se van a quedar sorprendidos de lo que alcanzaste pero solamente tú sabrás la verdad. Ningún sueño es posible sin dedicación y mucho trabajo. No esperes que la vida te de nada gratis, eso tiene que salir del sudor de tu frente. ¡Acuérdate de esto!" "*Never place too much attention on your little friends, not even when they laugh or criticize you. Quietly separate yourself from them in order to concentrate on your dreams. One of these days, they will be surprised at what you accomplished, but only you will know the truth. No dreams are possible without dedication and a lot of work. Don't expect life to give you anything for free, but instead from the sweat from your brow. Remember that.*"

These early life lessons were eventually to become important cornerstones in my life's work. Changing myself before attempting to change the lives of others proved to be especially difficult and challenging.

Taking a long hard look inside the self is not always a pretty or pleasant site, especially when certain life experiences at different intervals in life, were driven by the need for power and possession. Even more frightening is the realization of moving through life without a set of beliefs that involved a larger human calling or purpose, but instead reduces one to the monotony of work, engaged in meaning-less interactions with others, consumed by the need for economic gain, title, and self-importance.

For me, examining these thoughts required weeks alone quietly involved in an inner assessment of my ideas, at times uncertain about particular views and concepts, unable to determine which direction to take in my thinking. As I began jotting down these thoughts, the amount of crumpled paper scattered on the floor of my makeshift office at home revealed more of my frustrations than the progress of my thinking.

Writing was never an issue for me. I could scribble endlessly, ready to use quotes and references from published articles or information gained from the research of leading authorities. My motivation was not to publish or have my name attached to a document. This was my way of creating a mental record of thoughts that often crossed my mind in private moments of contemplation. This process of jotting down my thoughts, reflecting on them, and then determining the influences they had in my thinking slowly unfolded an important discovery about my behaviors, habits, and mental models that shaped my actions. Basic to my character makeup was an exaggerated fear of feeling alone and irrelevant in my relations to others. This discovery was crucial in shedding insight into the sense of loneliness that often interfered with my abilities to concentrate, and on occasion triggering anxiety and even panic attacks.

Taking action in changing these outcomes was not only an important step in working towards self-transformation. It placed me in greater control of what I most wanted. While there were no guarantees from changing my perspectives and outlooks, the idea of learning to take charge of my life was an exciting alternative to the realities facing me at the time.

Scary as it appeared at first, I came to accept the realization of no longer needing to rely on others to protect and counsel me along the way. The only obstacle standing between the former me and my new evolving self was in commanding responsibility for my actions and taking the first step towards altering the truths and beliefs that had been guiding me for so long. The moment had come to replace them with new, more meaningful alternatives. Instead of expecting the worst outcomes from my efforts, I began learning to believe that only good things would happen to me. Rather than distrusting others, I began learning to trust myself. Instead of letting the potential for setbacks evolve into hesitation and eventually a failure to act, I learned to make adjustments and improvements while reaching out for new life goals.

In the process of pursuing these changes in my life's journey, a new, more invigorating social reality emerged. One that gave me a much needed boost in self-confidence, put the controls to maneuver my life direction directly in my hands, and, more importantly, one that allowed me a freedom to craft a quality of life of purpose and relevancy.

The most important realization was arriving at the conclusion that life offered choices. I could choose to remain in a world of fixed structures and systems with clearly defined pathways to career opportunities and the prospects of achieving upper income levels. Alternatively, I could choose to form my own world of opportunities and successful outcomes, with no real guarantees of achieving them. One world assigned me to the life of a minority operating in a majority culture, hoping to eventually reach the top, but that world was also preparing me to accept less as the consolation prize for inclusion. In the other world, a reality of my making, there were no barriers, ceilings, or limitations to the possibilities of achieving the goals that were important to me. In the process, however, I had to accept the glaring possibilities that there were no guarantees for my efforts. I could either choose to operate in larger realities created and controlled by others or spend the remainder of my life crafting my own realities.

At times my friends would go over the definition of insanity when kidding with me about my work. "It's like a person continuing to expect a different outcome after first reading the final chapter of a book," Tootie, one of the NHI's original founders, would say. I already knew the outcome, the end-result of following particular pathways. Expecting a different outcome by remaining in an environment that undervalued my identity and capacity to contribute would be equivalent to insanity. There was no choice left except to construct new pathways to follow that not only would give me purpose and relevance, but also would resonate among those driven by similar needs. For me there had to be much more gained from the experience of life than having a job or business, being married, having children, attending church on Sundays, and growing satisfied with the general routines of day–to-day living. I felt that the human mind was equipped with the capacity to deal with much more.

It took time to realize and appreciate that the social realities of entire communities could be changed. My parents had done it in Magnolia, one of the most violent and feared communities of Houston. Through numerous activities that included sports, arts, music, cultural celebrations, civic work, and special events that brought out the best in young people, an entire community changed from seeing itself as spiritually, culturally, and socially broken to competing at the top of most endeavors. More important than the countless trophies and awards they received for their achievements was their trans-formation.

De Zavala Park had become much more than a place for recreation, being around friends, and playing sports. An entirely new culture of thinking had been injected and a different way of approaching life had been introduced. To approach life using the same outlooks, beliefs, and truths that guided my everyday interactions with life was indeed similar to reading a book by first reading the final chapter. The outcomes had already been clearly determined. What was needed instead was retrofitting myself with an altogether different set of social lenses and outlooks, based on also arming myself with an entirely new set of truths and beliefs. Rather than constantly looking to others for ideas and direction, my first step was to start relying on my own inherent capacity to imagine, craft, and propose different concepts and possibilities. Instead of quietly waiting for others to point the way for me to follow, I began testing my will and determination to act and pursue different pathways. And rather than allowing the prospect of possible failure to paralyze or delay me, I substituted faith and the lessons that come from doing my best to pursue a life mission that gave me a profound and enduring sense of human purpose that extended beyond my personal ambitions.

I believe that most all of us are caricatures of what we believe the world wants us to be. At least we start that way. My pathway to the future was linear in every sense of the word. Playing basketball in college was my way of getting a higher education. At first, my career plans were to become a high school basketball coach and maybe even try my hand at collegiate level sports. The sudden death of my brother Roy and the prospects of him in a vegetative state as a result of the multiple injuries he received changed my career path to special education. After-wards, I joined the Great Society Programs of the late President Lyndon B. Johnson to help fight poverty. Eventually I ended up in a government career position with state government. I envisioned my development as getting a college education, landing a secure job, getting married, having a family, and eventually retiring. Never before my 30th birthday did I stop to question who I had become in the process. There was no reason to raise questions. What mattered was playing golf on weekends, going on summer vacations, staying close to my boss, occasionally having dinner with friends, and being part of little league and tap dancing as my children grew.

In my early and middle thirties, something much more profound started stirring within me, something with a much deeper sense of emotion. I didn't particularly like the answers to the questions I started asking myself. Dad one day reminded me to decide once and for all if I was going to be Latino or convert totally to a mainstream life. He reassured me that I would always be his son either way. No matter how much I tried otherwise, I began changing inside. At times I grew filled with anger at allowing myself to drift from a culture I had so dearly loved as a child. We had previously spoken mostly Spanish at home. My best friends were my cousins. We attended at all Latino church where the sermons were conducted completely in Spanish. My best friends in the neighborhood live across and down the street. Even as a young man, going out meant dancing with girls at a nearby club where only Mexican music was played.

From the moment I stepped into college life, all of this changed suddenly and I began to alter every-thing about me. How I dressed, where I decided to live, and where I socialized all began to transform. It was all too apparent to me that it was not the world that had changed, it was me, and not necessarily for the better. Today, nothing makes me happier than to speak Spanish every day, have lunch with friends who share a similar world with me, and be part of four children whose spouses range from Texas to Mexico and Argentina. An entire new reality has emerged in the Nieto household where even the little ones conduct themselves completely in Spanish and English. Who am I today is a person who is culturally at ease, who travels throughout Latin America and has friends in most every major city in the United States. Who I am is wearing Tejano boots, listening to Tejano music and imagining my Dad harmonizing with me to Hijo del Pueblo or watching Mom smile and shed tears when listening to her all-time favorite song, Solamente Una Vez. It's a new world out there, a world that is comforting, familiar, and accepts me uncon-ditionally for who I am.

In the end, my mother's counsel was right. There are universal powers that exist for everyone to make part of their lives. All of us have the innate capacities to construct endless concepts and possibilities when we allow our minds to imagine without self-imposed ceilings, boundaries, and other limitations. All of us have the ability to call on the courage needed to step forward into the unknown if we can lay aside our needs to predict outcomes. All of us can wander through the confusion of unraveling complex thoughts and rambling endlessly through the wilderness of life. In pursuing important life dreams, we must be anchored by a deeply rooted faith that makes acting on ideas the only means of clarifying our direction in pursuing our own self-crafted destination. The lesson that my mother ultimately wanted me to understand was that change does not begin with changing the world that exists outside of us, but rather from consistent and deter-mined efforts to change from within. In calling on faith to change ourselves, we also begin taking the first initial steps in constructing the building blocks needed to begin crafting new realities, new truths, and new beliefs to guide our lives.

Creating something that represented lasting value and usefulness that to Latino youth has always been underneath my work at the Institute. An old friend by the name of Dr. Jorge Lara-Braud once came by the Institute as a presenter in a "legends project." Jorge, as a Presbyterian minister, had been instru-mental in establishing the La Raza Unida

Conference in 1967 at the newly opened Kennedy High School in San Antonio, Texas. This was the birthplace of "El Movimiento," as it was later known.

During a presentation to undergraduate NHIers, Jorge observed that he understood all too well the underlying intent of the Institute, but wasn't quite sure whether it could be achieved. Twenty-five years later, he was a recipient of the Institute's Life Time Achievement Award for his long and dedicated service. By now, however, he was well into his late 70s and was visibly suffering the devastating effects of Parkinson's. Still, he was courageous enough to make some closing comments that were to become his last public remarks before his death two weeks later. During his speech, Jorge told a story of Archbishop Flores from San Antonio who visited the Vatican years before to meet with Pope John Paul II. It was there that the word "Chicano" became part of the conversation because the term was completely alien to His Holiness.

Jorge used the occasion of this story to describe the work of NHI as being an instrument that creates the cavaliers of an identity that keeps growing and developing. In the end, Jorge concluded that Latinos have arrived at a time when we have been able to "claim the right to be who we are." Through these brief remarks and in spite of his ailing condition, Jorge captured the aim in my heart that eventually led to the creation of an institute that will continue for many years to come.

7.

SELF REFLECTION AND CHANGE

Who we are and wish to become as a community cannot be left to the perceptions of others, but instead the truths, beliefs, and images of our own making.

Two steps are vital for those who choose to play visible and intentional leadership roles in Latino community life. First, we must work towards gaining a keen understanding and awareness of the multiple factors that shape our social perspectives, values, and beliefs from the mental models we use in our dealings with others. Secondly, we also must learn to assume full responsibility for the decisions to lead through our determination to achieve, willingness to act, and mental focus required to reach our intended destinations.

As humans, we don't grow up in unbiased environments. Brothers, sisters, cousins, parents, schoolteachers, priests, ministers, close friends, and so many more participate in shaping and influencing our understanding of the world around us. T.V. does the same, as does the music we hear and the information we read in newspapers, magazines, books, etc. Together they help to form our ethos, our national character, and the beliefs that guide us through life. They help to form the views that give us a sense of shared membership, a collective identity and destiny, and a purpose in the societies where we live.

Taking aggressive steps to alter and evolve a new, more compelling national identity has to rank at the top of our priorities as a community in order to achieve new outcomes in the future. In redesigning our character, we may develop a calling that unites, and make community engagement a fulfilling and self-educating experience. The sheer size of a Latino community that is growing at an unprecedented rate will not cause a positive shift by itself. Latinos not only need to be concerned with projecting community images that correspond with an emerging 21st century world, but also to be in control of the images we wish to project as a dynamic and modern community.

Until now, those images have been constructed and advanced by outside interests. For example, being a "minority" or "person of color" is not a social image advanced by Latinos. The social connotations of these images devalue the Latino community and make it a liability to a larger society that demands remedial attention and interventions. By reconstructing the current day image and assigning it a completely different value and meaning, new social expectations are automatically placed into motion that not only can impact the thinking of the future Latino community in general, but more specifically, issue a different calling and challenge that younger Latinos can be motivated to pursue.

Latino elected officials, educational leaders, and heads of community and business organizations will soon occupy the landscape of leadership in many of majority-Latino communities across the nation. However, the absence of resources, a widening social divide within the Latino community, and a continued insistence on social models that reward assimilation and emphasize careerism as the path to the American Dream will remain obstacles to a community that requires visionaries more than it requires professionals.

Throughout its many years of work with educationally advanced high school Latinos across the nation, the NHI has tracked and evaluated the dynamics of the current social model for high-ability Latinos. Inevitably, the perceptions and values that mainstream culture has impressed upon these young individuals often places Latinos in a regressive experience in comparison to other American ethnic communities.

One method of tracking and evaluating Latino community perceptions comes from a game simulation that involves high school sophomores and juniors. Participants from across the U. S. and from different walks of life are asked to respond to a series of questions in which they make specific choices in response to various community challenges.

To start the activity, a senior trainer invites four students who are different in physical appearance to the front of a youth audience that ranges from 150-230 participants. Each of the students is given a role to represent one of four ethnic communities usually Latino, African-American, Asian-American, and Caucasian. The trainer begins by describing an imaginary scenario in which the audience is asked to indicate their individual choices by raising their hands in response to specific questions.

"Let's make believe for a moment." The trainer begins by posing the first question: "Let's say that I'm a very old, wealthy person who leaves a will that grants an inheritance of one million dollars to each of you immediately payable upon my death. In my will, however, a stipulation is made that in order to keep the inheritance; each of you must invest in only one of the four ethnic groups with the opportunity of either doubling the money in 30 days or having to relinquish it altogether. In which group would you have the greatest confidence?

Over the last 25 years of asking the same question to different audiences of Latino youth who represent different regions across the nation, different nationalities, and different socio-economic back-grounds, their responses historically have followed the same patterns without any significant shifts or changes.

Almost always, the overwhelming majority of the students make Asian-Americans their first choice, followed by Caucasians second, African-Americans third and Latinos last.

The second question follows.

"Let's pretend that time has moved forward and now you are married and have a couple of young children. Imagine vacationing in a crowded city somewhere in the world and suddenly a power surge occurs, causing all the city lights to go out. Let's further imagine that the city lacks transportation services, forcing you and your family to walk through the darkness across several neighborhoods to eventually reach your hotel. Which of these groups would you trust to get you back safely?"

The students think for a few seconds before raising their hands. Students once again express a significant preference by choosing Asian-Americans first, followed by Caucasians, with Latinos and African-Americans interchangeably selected third and last.

The third and final question is asked.

"This time," the trainer begins, "let's say that you have misspent your inheritance with less than five thousand dollars remaining, and wish to make a lasting contribution to a family member. Imagine an aging grandmother who lives in a home with a leaky roof that you want to repair. You want someone who does good, solid job, but doesn't cost a lot of money. Which one of the ethnic groups would you choose first, second, third, and last to fix the roof in a thorough manner at the lowest possible cost?"

This time the students significantly reverse their choices, selecting Latinos first, Blacks second, Caucasians third, and Asians last.

After completing the activity, the students discuss their choices and describe the underlying beliefs, assumed truths, and social outlooks that led them to make each choice. When questioned about why the majority of the students selected Asian-Americans to make the right investment using their supposed inheritance, the term "smart" dominated the explanation of their choices. In the second scenario, the students chose Caucasians, describing the social perception that Anglos could be "trusted" the most to get them back to the hotel safely.

The students' response to the third question uncovered a largely shared perception that Latinos can be hard-working, reliable people who do good work, and whose services easily can be acquired for
a relatively low cost.

Beyond the surface beliefs and truths that tend to guide the thinking of young Latinos regarding race and culture, the more disturbing revelations have to do with the conclusions they tend to draw in defining their individual identities and associations with Latino culture. Despite their expressed wishes to see their fellow Latinos lead more active and productive lives across all spectrums of community life, their shared beliefs and truths describe an altogether different set of social perspectives and outlooks. They lack confidence in a community of people who, to them, express little willingness, determination, or vision to change.

The perceptions and outlooks expressed by these bright, academically advanced Latinos have remained consistent for nearly 30 years, despite being from different socioeconomic backgrounds, regions, and cultural origins. The majority of students are competitive, intelligent, and envision themselves attending our nation's most rigorous and sought-after universities. They also express a high level of interest in eventually playing leadership roles in Latino community life. An alarming disconnect consequentially emerges between individual aspirations to attend these institutions and play key roles in Latino community life, paired with an inherent lack of trust in the Latino community to change itself.

The discussion follows with several questions: "How can you see yourself playing leadership roles in a community that you see as being essentially backward?"

"Is it possible that you are saying all the right things about your individual futures right now, but really never intend to become actively involved in Latino community life once you finish college and become a working professional or business owner?"

"Are you preparing to make your final departure with the ultimate intent of making Latino life your exit, not your destination community?"

Training in community self-inquiry provides future leaders with the means to make distinctions between community operating beliefs and outlooks that no longer should remain functional and possibly could prove detrimental to the psychological well-being of the future Latino community if preserved. Developing their capacities in self-inquiry arms these future leaders with the ability for self-study and review of the multiple operating beliefs that Latinos tend to use as the mental models that allow them to socially define themselves. These capacities also guide them to take strategic steps in injecting new thoughts and concepts that can alter community self-perception and strengthen prospects for collaborative endeavor.

Dealing with these complex and sensitive issues has been one of the initial steps taken by the NHI in introducing community leadership to young Latinos. Through similar processes, they are guided to reflect on their own life experiences with the intent of pinpointing underlying beliefs and truths that have formed the social lenses through which they tend to perceive life and the roles they envision for them-selves, and their particular opinion, and attitudes towards others.

In training youth to unravel questions of perception, they are able to make key and important distinctions between truths and beliefs passed on to them in their formative years by parents and other important family members, as well as those gained from their daily encounters and interactions with their external world. Recognizing the difference between the familial and external forces allows one to forge together their own life perceptions. Creating a self-made philosophy to guide oneself becomes an important realization and an introductory under-standing to reality formation. It also has a profound impact on one's identity formation and worldviews.

As leaders, we must attempt to gain an understanding of our development, to review the circumstances of our conditions, and to measure the extent to which these influences shape our lives. Self-inquiry allows young Latinos to critically review their nurtured state, their imposed state, and their evolving self-crafted state. The NHI's programs act as a "disruptive experience" by stirring self-inquiry and moving participants to attempt to make sense of the influences that are shaping their beliefs and individual identities. The NHI experience questions the status quo of our individual belief systems. It forces students to look inward, instead of outward, for answers to their many unanswered questions. It allows them to reflect, analyze, and distinguish beliefs that no longer represent value to their development and may perhaps be harmful to their future development. It gives them a basis to incorporate new beliefs that are more in keeping with their preferred life directions. Above all, self- inquiry allows young people to concentrate on the sacred, the beliefs that they embrace as fundamental truths. In doing so, they are consciously recognizing permanent outlooks and guide posts that they choose to use in conducting their lives and forming lifelong relations with others.

Once a person consciously begins to change from within, the rest follows naturally new mental models, new behaviors, outlooks, attitudes, habits, and patterns. For me, this change came after letting go of my sense of entitlement. For years, my operating belief was that it was the government's responsibility to level the playing fields of opportunity and equality. Never did it occur to me that first change had to occur in my own attitudes and outlooks. When first starting the NHI, I would sit for hours in my home office waiting for the telephone to ring, for someone to call with an opportunity. I rarely saw myself constructing a widget, a service, or product that potentially could benefit someone else. I was waiting to be discovered, for someone to notice my worth and value. Learning to think of myself as a valued and worthy person had to come from me, not anyone else. Regrettably, what I discovered was that credentials and college degrees realistically meant little in the business world. These are the mental shifts that have to occur inside the psyche of the individual before any meaningful progress begins to occur. Change from within has little to do with affirmative action, careers, or diversity in the work place.

Developing the capacities for personal self-encounters represents a crucial step in establishing the stage for transformation of the individual. Every-thing begins with the self, extends into larger groups, and finally, realizes in communities. Inquiry serves to unfold an understanding of the key roles an individual can play in strategically determining the direction of larger populations. In questioning Latinos in respect to community transformation, one may search for a new, more invigorating identity and national character consistent within a modern 21st century world. To dwell in the historic and romantic notions of identities no longer relevant to a modern day world is to remain stuck in an anachronistic quagmire, a self-aggrandized portrait that bears little resemblance to the truth and offers little usefulness to the constant shaping and adaptations the individual must undergo to maintain pace with the demands of evolving, changing environments.

Through discussions that question, challenge, and confront existing beliefs of the youth who engage the NHI, reality formation is introduced as an alive and breathing phenomenon consisting of a multitude of social forces with the power of influencing, altering, and shaping the beliefs and truths that guide entire societies. They also begin to gain an under-standing of the roles these social forces play in constructing their own individual identities, views, beliefs, preferences, perspectives, outlooks, practices, patterns, attitudes, and habits on a daily basis. They learn to understand change as a constantly evolving process that begins with shifts that can be imperceptible, subtle, and sometimes undetectable. They realize, however, that eventually they can take control in driving entire groups of people to undergo significant changes in their overall beliefs, culture, identity, and even national character. In the end, they learn to construct a framework that provides them with the means for social analysis.

The training provided through the NHI grants individuals a first-time look at the forces in their lives that brought them to adopt the beliefs that guide their identities and individual life directions. They review influences from their early childhood that were mostly transferred by loved ones. They inspect the perspectives they receive through the literature they read, television programs they watch, churches they attend, objects they purchase, and views of those they listen to. In essence, the NHI community examines the influences that form the internal and external worlds in which we operate. Through their experiences, students realize that while there are both family and external influences that shape and impact their lives, they too can craft their own social influences and life destinations. By working towards this eventual goal and outcome, we begin to gain control over the pathways we wish to pursue. Through this examination, we begin to explore how to lead purposeful lives within communities and beyond careers, social status, and the need for prestige and importance.

Many years ago, I would remind young people in Houston that leadership ultimately meant learning to "lead your own ship." Learning to lead your own ship is a person's first step in self-realization. If one cannot manage their own affairs, aggressively pursue their dreams, get up from setbacks and disillusionments, and remain focused on a goal until it is accomplished, then they cannot lead anyone else, no matter the title or position one holds. People learn to evaluate their leadership capacities not by watching others, but by first looking inwardly and asking themselves important questions. Do I act on what I say I'm going to do or just do a lot of talking? Can I delay my needs for instant gratification until the goal I'm pursuing is reached? Do I get off the horse when I'm knocked down, or do I consistently get back up again? Am I willing to pay the price of success by keeping on the task? Do I make excuses for not staying focused or becoming easily distracted? Do I jump from project to project, eventually overwhelming myself to the extent that nothing succeeds or works? Do I learn from the mistakes of others? Do I seek counsel and advice while holding myself responsible for my own actions?

"Sólo tú puedes controlar tu vida, no los otros, hijo. Sólo tú puedes poner el esfuerzo necesario para alcanzar tus metas.

Guarda silencio y solamente concéntrate en lo que quieres lograr, en lo que quieres alcanzar en la vida." "Only you can control your life, not others, son. The effort required to reach your goals only can come from you. Be quiet and concentrate only on what you want to reach, what you intend in life."

Recalling the life lessons of my parents and paying close attention to their advice has been among my most important accomplishments.

8.

CONCEPT OF REALITY FORMATION

*There exists in all of us a powerful capacity
to call on our imagination and
creativity to take us to outcomes
beyond our own expectations.*

*"Hay cuatro cosas que tienes que usar en tu vida, hijo,""There are four
things that you must use in life, son,"*Dad reminded me one day
while sitting on our front porch in Houston.

*"La primera es la que ya viene en tu sangre, desde allá, tus antepasados.
La segunda es la vida diaria, experiencias aquí con tu familia, pláticas
que te han ayudado a que seas lo que eres hoy. Después, viene la vida
exterior, el mundo donde vas a vivir y vivirás el resto de tu vida. Y por
último, la vida que tú quieres vivir, que tú formarás y que será tu
identidad". "One is the thing that al-ready exists in your veins that
comes from those who came before you. The other is your daily life
experiences here with your family; conversations that have helped shape
you. Afterwards comes the external life, the world in which you live and
will continue to live for the rest of your life. And finally, comes the life
you wish to live, that you craft and will become your identity."*

It would take years, generations of reflection and engaging
the world for me to finally gain an understanding of my
father's counsel – he was a man who made analyzing life and
self- reflection his lifelong hobby. Many times I would see
him sitting on the porch or at the table staring into space,
engaged in deep personal thought. These moments were not
occasional, but numerous. Much more than being a father, a
husband, a brother, and a provider, Santos Nieto was first
and foremost a thinker, a person who through the years had
evolved his own philosophy and vision of life. It was not

unusual for him to allow his innermost emotions to get the better of him. There were times when I would see him tear up or gently be held in mom's comforting arms while they sat together at the kitchen table.

Both of my parents had endured years of suffering, of having to do without, "pasando vergüenzas" (experiencing embarrassments) as Mom used to remind us. Both of my parents grew up at the turn of the 20th century: dad being born in 1903, mom in 1910. While dad had a father, he never really knew him because he had gone off to war during the Mexican revolution of 1910. At 13, dad's mother died during the Great Influenza, immediately followed by his sister. Alone, he left for Houston to join his older brother of 12 years, where he worked sixteen-hour days laying track for the Southern Pacific Railroad. Dad never got over having to fight just because he had a darker skin and was Mexican American. He never forgot constantly being harassed by the police, being turned down from jobs or relegated to the less paying jobs simply because of his ethnicity. It was in following his mother's counsel of going to church on Sundays that he would meet Esther Alfaro, who would become his wife of 63 years.

Mom's circumstances were not that different from dad's, except in the situations that surrounded her childhood. In the early 1900s, life for the majority of Mexicans residing in the United States was one of extreme poverty. Mom's mother, Emilia was shunned from the family for having a child out of wedlock. As was the practice back then, mom was placed under the protective care of her strict grandmother, while Emilia took jobs that were mostly reserved for men. She picked cotton from dusk to dawn during the blistering heat of summers, drove mule teams to plant crops during spring, and cooked for hungry field workers at night, all before returning to her home to clean and tend to her growing daughter Esther, and her five younger siblings.

Esther Nieto never stopped caring for her mother, especially considering the circumstances of their lives. As a child, she faithfully followed her grandmother's expectations of making religion a major part of her life. At ten, my mother had to clean house, bathe her younger brothers and sister before going to bed, wash their clothes for school and at dusk, bring back kindling for the wood-burning stove and late night dinners for the field workers.

Mom never forgot the toll these responsibilities had on her emotionally and psychologically; picking cotton for pennies a day, never having enough food for herself and her younger siblings, and being forced to accept the social discomforts of hand-me-downs from older cousins and church families while constantly moving around.

For both of my parents, imagination and creativity became the only options available of giving them a way out; the possibility of achieving a better life. The old saying "necessity is the mother of invention" never was more true for two individuals who grew up in the dusty fields of South Texas and found themselves in the hostile environment of severe racial prejudice as teenagers in Houston. It was there, in their attempts to create a better future, that they discovered another character element in their makeup. It began with human will the capacity to stand tall against the odds of life. It continued with using imagination and creativity to step beyond one's own self-expectations, armed only with a "can do" spirit and the resiliency to withstand the looming prospect of failure.

The lessons of my parent's journey unfold a scenario not too different from a significant number of modern day Latinos. For a growing, diverse, and dynamic U.S. Latino community, this moment in our history represents a timely challenge and opportunity to make significant changes in the lives we intend to carry out within the American experience. All of us, from the moment of birth, begin individual journeys through space and time that carry two definitive outcomes; a beginning and an end. In between, we have no choice in the selection of our parents or the number of siblings accompanying us along the way. In the beginning, we have little knowledge regarding the pathways we individually pursue. For some, life is a simple, momentary flicker. Others continue living longer, extended life spans. Some run into misfortunes. Their journeys are interrupted by disease, accidents, wars, and other life-ending tragedies.

Where we live, and the conditions that surround us at birth, are not of our making or choosing. We play no role in determining race, cultural heritage, physical characteristics, gender, intellectual potential, or the extent to which we are mentally and physically healthy.

What is known is that along the way, we are socialized as a community by numerous people who assume responsibility for transmitting certain views of life through particular social prisms that are con-veyed to us throughout our lifetimes. Some are societal truths presented as being undeniable facts and written into social laws. Others are more transient in nature, often in response to modern day phenomena and trends. Most of these prisms, however, are generational and emanate from the combined life histories and human experiences that pass through time. They are the combination of shared life experiences that draw us to perceive and interpret life through particular social lenses, passed on from generation to generation, from family to family and on to the child.

These perceived truths and realities, combined with their strength, constancy, and resiliency to the tests of time, form the boundaries and guidelines used by Latino families. They become collective social maps that guide us in our daily interactions and the social trajectories we choose to take. They become measures that allow us to form assessments as a community and as individual members to forecast the probabilities of our success and the risk-potential of our decisions.

The combination of these adopted and learned community truths and beliefs is transformed into living realities that not only weld together our world views and define our national identity, but also influence how others view us. From a Latino point of view, they play significant roles in establishing the social boundaries in which we learn to feel comfortable and secure. They shape the economic landscape in which we decide to pursue our livelihoods. They help form our individual identities and the value we assign to our identity as a community bound together by language, culture, religion, and similarities in histories. In the end, they shape our social perspectives and outlooks, our relations with one another, and the attitudes we assume in managing our daily lives.

The challenge for the new emerging Latino leadership of the 21st century, however, not only lies in accepting the notion that change is vital to the future health and well-being of the Latino com-munity, but also in determining the scope of change that must be pursued. The formation of a new, modern day reality is not only important, but also crucial given the current educational condition and trajectory of Latinos in general. The Latino com-munity is currently defined by its un-paralleled, increasingly diverse growth, the fact that Latinos are largely a consumer community with little economic wealth or political social capital, and the certainty that Latinos are becoming the majority community in various strategic regions of the nation. To perform less than our capacity or ignore the moment is to neither understand the challenge nor appreciate the opportunity to make lasting changes in ways that we, as Latinos, historically have seen ourselves and determine how best to lead our lives.

Changing and redefining com-munity realities, however, require a determined and sustained effort over extended periods of time. It includes no longer accepting popularly held public perceptions that have previously guided our identity as a community. Views that define us as being the fastest growing "minority" in the nation or the "sleeping giant" must be seen as inappropriate social markers that position us at the bottom of society. The same can be said about self-deprecating descriptions used in talking about ourselves, descriptions that connote a com-munity of under-developed or incapable individuals who cannot appreciate the opportunities in front of us.

We also must grow beyond the notion of being a community unable to organize into common endeavors, instead remaining in tribal-like groups continually competing with one another. These self-imposed images of ourselves serve little purpose other than to marginalize who we are, reducing our value in comparison to other cultures. Left uncontested, these public impressions assume a life of their own. They become believable truths and realities that weaken our external projection and internal image, dampen our hopes and aspirations, and make advancement improbable.

The public perceptions that formed our national identity and the underlying beliefs that led to its creation are not easily erased.

Opinions can operate like human viruses. They develop through time, infect the mind, and become difficult to expel. Opinions shape the human psyche, frame thought, and lead entire communities to believe that certain fates were destined to occur beyond our capacities to influence and control.

The dawning of the 21st century allows us not only to re-think our directions as a community, but also to form new beliefs and truths that can strengthen cooperation among our-selves and make sustained common endeavor possible. As Latinos we must assume responsibility for being the chief architects of the changes we wish to make and the goals we want to achieve. No one else is qualified to assist us but ourselves. No one else lives in our collective minds but us.

When the National Hispanic Institute was first established in 1979, conventional wisdom led us to direct our efforts to the special problems and challenges faced by low-income parents and their children. We argued another point of view on behalf of high potential youth. Back then, NHI's intent was to pursue funding from government agencies and private foundations. We never gave any thought to the implications of our intended aims, except to help guide young men and women from the Austin area in their transition from high school to college.

It wouldn't be until the late 1980s and early 90s that we began to realize the existence of an outlook on that cut across urban, suburban, and rural youth. By that point, however, the success of our high school leadership programs like the Lorenzo de Zavala Youth Legislative Session had already spread to New Mexico, Colorado, the Midwest, and California. By this time we also considered ourselves a national organization with a broad vision, calling to increase and expand the supply of future community leader-ship in response to the nationally depleted and thinning Latino leadership base. What we found during private discussions with the youth was both unsettling and troublesome.

First, the majority of the young men and women didn't see themselves as returning back to their communities upon graduating from college. Going to college was their way of escape, leaving behind a community that they for the most part felt was backwards and burdened with numerous problems of gang violence, drug abuse, and poverty in general. Making donations to community causes and projects, after establishing themselves in their respective careers, stood for giving back.

Second, many of these high school students were willing be seen as minorities and disadvantaged if it meant getting help through various forms of scholarships and other forms of financial support for their undergraduate and graduate studies. So long as someone else was footing the bill and college studies was being made accessible, social labeling didn't matter. It was merely the price and sacrifice required to get ahead. In fact, many justified no longer being able to speak Spanish well by submitting that English mastery and navigating mainstream culture was far more important than speaking a "foreign language." Some saw Spanish as a language that was only useful on occasions with grandparents, if they were still around.

Third, leadership was understood from a representation point of view rather than playing an active role in the daily affairs of Latino community life. Some looked forward to serving on prestigious public and private boards and commissions for purposes of representing Latino views. From an impact point of view, most saw themselves as broadening opportunities for other Latinos in their attempts to also access advance their interests. But they also saw these roles as opportunities to further their professional aspirations and demonstrate their skills, so they could hopefully move further up in their career pursuits. Few, if any, expressed any attraction to community involvement and being visible, active participants in the daily lives of families either formally or informally.

The more disturbing finding during these encounters with students in the 1990s was not so much in coming to grip with these views; it was in accepting the impressions these young people seemingly had regarding the work of NHI. To them, the NHI's entire mission and calling was not merely a collective representation of these views, but also the means through which they as young people could expect to realize their dreams as participants and members. Why else did we want to them to go Harvard, Southwestern University, Boston University, Rice University, Stanford, Notre Dame, Duke, and the like? Why else did we want them to become people involved in law, architecture, engineering, education, and business development? And weren't we determining success by the same mainstream measures and standards?

It wouldn't be for several years that the answer would come. By then, my mother was 93 years old. Dad had since passed away in 1993, nine years earlier. Mom and I spent many hours together afterwards, often going for long drives in the hills and winding roads of central Texas. Springtime in late March was an especially attractive time. We would leave early in the morning and stop somewhere not too far from a rocky spring with hills covered in Texas bluebonnets and Indian paintbrushes. Anytime we got together, talking about religion was expected in our conversations.

"¿Cómo ves esto, hijo?" "How do you view this, son," She asked one time during those special moments together.

"¿Cuál es el propósito de la iglesia? ¿Salvar almas o cambiar vidas?" *"What is the purpose of church? Save souls or change lives?"*

There we were again, one more time, involved in an intense discussion that required hours of conversation. And customary to these talks, there was never a right or wrong, only the sharing of ideas. Dad had been gone for some time, but the tradition continued. Mom was asking a critically important question, a question of perception, impression, and comparison. There were no easy answers to her query, only possibilities.

I finally, after all these years, understood their work; an effort that spanned 49 years of working intimately with countless youth and families until both of them finally retired. An answer was being gifted to me by my remaining parent. Their work had been driven by efforts that inspired change, rather than efforts to counsel young people to change. They saw value, possibilities, and greatness in every young person who entered their lives; from those with troubled pasts to young men and women with amazing potential.

She explained, *"Muy pocos escuchan a aquel que demanda cambios. Es aquel que inspira quien produce cambios y también quien cambia vidas." "To the person who demands change, few ever listen. The person who inspires change, also changes lives."*

An answer had finally been provided, elusive as it had been for years. It was all in our mindsets, our perceptions of ourselves, and the perceptions of the community we wish to serve. My mother and father carefully crafted environments that attracted and inspired young men and women to become engaged, to enjoy the experience, and to want others to share in the same. T hey made certain that these young people repeatedly had positive experiences. They insisted on preparation and leaving no stone unturned when competing. What others thought was not even considered. It was what the youth at the park thought of themselves that mattered. Everyone was a stakeholder, a policy maker, and a valued member. Success in the community was a standard, a common expectation. These were the basic ingredients that made new realities and paradigms possible. Instead of allowing others to determine the identity of youth from DeZavala Park, this responsibility was handed over to the park youth to determine through their actions and insistence on succeeding.

Dad would often remind me, *"Recuerda, hijo, que si un muchacho está inspirado no hay pobreza, discriminación o racismo que lo detenga.*

90

Cuando una persona está convencida de que puede, crea su propia realidad y dirección. Dedícate a ser la persona que inspire y mantenga la visión al frente de los ojos de la gente. El resto viene de ellos."
"Remember son, for an inspired young person, not poverty, discrimination, or racism can get in the way. When convinced that he can, a person creates his own reality and direction. Dedicate yourself as the person who inspires and keeps the vision in front of their eyes. The rest comes from them."

Mom died a year after our conversation and is buried next to Dad in Houston. My brother Albert followed shortly after, leaving only me as the sole surviving member of five. Their legacy and life lessons, however, remain as alive in the work of the Institute as if they were there present here today. The next step is clear. We have the capacities, calling, imagination, and will to realize the message of investing in our global community.

9.

NEW BELIEFS THE FIRST STEP

Change does not come from wishing
or being cautious, but instead taking crucial
and permanent steps to craft a new identity
as individuals, as a community,
and the world we choose to surround us.

The greatest task in the cultivation of today's growing Latino community lies in providing our youth with new, realistic, effective social models to guide their individual and collective success. As early as 1981, when the NHI conducted its first Young Leaders Conference, the operating theory was that new, more dynamic, and appealing social models were needed to attract high school Latinos to consider alternative pathways for success and inclusion that were different than those in existence. At the time, we did not realize that it would take us years to craft new possibilities that would, in turn, demand additional years of development, testing, and evaluation with Latino students from different age groups, various regions of the nation, and diverse cultural backgrounds.

In the past, young Latinos have had two primary models to guide their development. Some have relied upon social models available in street-oriented urban lifestyles. These in-variably lead to low educational attainment, unproductive use of time, and a day-to-day existence that fosters dependency and yields meager resources for their daily needs. Others have assimilated into the American mainstream. Being accepted, however, tends to result in marginalization or, in some instances, the questioning of an individual's value. Youth are assigned a minority identity, given an unremarkable role in the workplace, and are informed by their surroundings to discard many semblances of their ethnic identities all as the price for gaining admission into a culture of "success." Inspiring the creation of alternative social models by and for Latino youth has shaped the mission and work of the NHI since 1979.

The concept of Third Reality as a working strategy eventually emerged as a viable option in the evolution of the NHI's work. However, it took years of experimentation, reflection, discussion, and alteration to create a combined approach that was both age-appropriate and effective in igniting a need for personal change.

Third Reality Revealed is based on the operating concept and belief that our identities largely are the product of two major life influences: First Reality, or the Nurtured State, represents the primary identity-forming experiences that shape the beliefs of the individual resulting from interactions with parents and other loved ones. Second Reality, or the Imposed State, represents experiences that shape the individual resulting from interactions with the external world.

The life lessons of First Reality generally come from the experiences of love, affection, loyalty, belonging, and kinship. It shapes the person's under-standing of the spiritual self and the capacities to express and share emotional bonds with others. It introduces anger and jealousy, sadness and exhilaration. First Reality in essence is the chief means through which the emotional and psychological makeup of the person is initially determined, forming the basic social framework and lenses to perceive and interpret the external world.

Second Reality, the Imposed State, represents the world's institutions, structures, regulations, standards, and means of evaluating the social value and usefulness of an individual.

Second Reality makes discriminating choices between people it prefers and those it rejects, between people who can serve its interests and those seen as potential liabilities. It is driven by inertia to sustain and promulgate existing social structures. It assigns value to individuals based on their capacities to succeed according to its standards along with their willingness to undergo vast personal change as the cost of attaining power, prestige, and status.

Third Reality, or the Self Crafted State, is neither a natural extension of First Reality or Second Reality, nor does it imply a particular lifestyle or point-of-view. The concept of Third Reality provides the individual with a means for social analysis to critically evaluate the operating beliefs and truths that guide personal outlooks, views, behaviors, patterns, practices, and habits. Utilizing a Third Reality approach, the person is able to selectively conduct individual assessments of the mental models used as references for personal decision making. They also are able to identify beliefs that no longer may be useful or even potentially if allowed to remain a part of their makeup. In this context, the responsibility for change becomes a proprietary right and responsibility of the person to craft the beliefs and truths that they feel are more in keeping with who they wish to become without the need for conformity to standards and measures outside of their control.

In practice, Third Reality resembles the current-day teaching theories and practices that fall under the heading of social constructivism. In the early 1900s Jean Piaget, a Swiss-born psychologist and philosopher, developed the argument that children gain knowledge from and attribute meaning to the accumulation of their daily life experiences.

Piaget delineated two mechanisms that, in his view, learners use to take in knowledge from infancy on. His early version of constructivism asserts that through the processes of assimilation and accommodation individuals construct new knowledge from their experiences. Infants absorb everything uncritically. Parents and older siblings define the meaning that infants and young children attribute to their unfolding experiences as they grow, explore, experiment, and discover. Over time, they develop what Piaget called a schema – a mental model for understanding the world and how it works and how they should interact with that world. In fact, schemas are internal mental representations of the external world. They are different in every society and culture. Schemas are, in other words, socially constructed.

In assimilating, people take in and incorporate new experiences into their preexisting mental models without changing the models themselves. This most often occurs when an individual's experiences and the meanings they attribute to those experiences are compatible with their existing schemas. In Piaget's view, people may assimilate flawed, incomplete, or distorted new information because the meaning attributed to new experiences may be based on insufficient awareness of particular facts, misunderstood information or advice, or in deciding that an event is unimportant. Piaget also believed that people change or distort their perceptions of their experiences to fit their existing internal schemas or representations.

According to Piaget's version of constructivism, accommodation is the process of adapting one's mental model or internal representation of the external world in order to take in new experiences that do not fit their previously existing schema. Accommodation is the mechanism through which a "failure" becomes a means for learning. When we assume that the world operates one way, but perceive that some undeniable reality violates (i.e. disconfirms) our expectations, our mental model noticeably fails us. By accepting and accommodating the new experience and restructuring our internal mental models, we learn something new. We modify old assumptions or incorporate new expectations. We change our beliefs about the way the world works. People also can learn from observing how others deal with their failures – but this is a less powerful learning.

Third Reality was designed as a concept for young people who recognize the need for personal development and realize the benefits they can achieve by making substantial changes in the way they conduct and manage their lives. The process of Third Reality as a means for critical self-evaluation fosters a heightened awareness and need for personal change as the requirement for self-advancement. The same benefits potentially could be realized when applying Third Reality to entire com-munities. Traditional methods of negotiating change and advancement no longer would rely on rigid hierarchies of leadership that tend to diffuse rather than excite involvement. Collaborative effort would become more the standard as opposed to observing the administrative misuse of protocol and procedures. The value of ideas would take precedence over title and position. More important, the focus of Third Reality would be in altering community perceptions and behaviors through the replacement of old operating beliefs with new ones that expand involvement and make change possible.

The generally poor rankings of Latino youth in their academic studies, their high school dropout rates, and similar low showings in their college completion rates are indicators that point to the absence of appropriate social models to guide Latino youth in U.S. community life. Social models that relegate young Latinos to minority status or define them socially as needing therapeutic intervention or special services create a deficit mindset rather than one that is uplifting and inspiring.

A Third Reality mindset provides Latino youth with a different social scale and set of standards to determine their

96

self-worth and value. As an asset-building concept, it gives students the tools they need for self-evaluation, for questioning operating truths that surround their development, and for making appropriate changes in the mental models they use to navigate their lives. As a living concept, Third Reality helps youth to dislodge themselves from operating truths they have learned to accept and use in guiding their development and, instead, replace them with more invigorating options that compel them to pursue higher standards of performance and self-expectations. In the end, the framework of Third Reality fosters a more productive young person. It guides youth away from a culture of minimum expectations to a culture of success that helps shape a more responsible, conscientious, and focused potential citizen and leader.

This strategy to community development has been the principal means of support that has led to the growth and expansion of the NHI throughout its thirty-one year history. Rather than rely on traditional sources of support such as grants, the NHI has historically looked to its constituents of Latino youth and their families for its primary means of mobilizing funding, supplying volunteers, and relying on leadership at community levels. Creativity, inventiveness, vision, and collaboration have played similar roles in the success of the NHI. No human attributes, however, have been more instrumental than imagination, faith, and the will to act. Without these three ingredients driving the mindsets and outlooks of the organization's leader-ship, the likelihood of growing over such a long period of time probably would not be possible. With them, everything has remained possible and reachable.

Third Reality frameworks arm young Latinos with the skills and capacities to make major changes in altering their personal life trajectories and to manage the challenging questions that emerge along the way. It represents the core concept of the NHI training curricula designs and the high-intensity learning experiences that youth enjoy through the organization's highly popular use of games. The approaches help remove barriers that prevent questions from being raised and often contradict the social perspectives, assumptions, beliefs, and expectations that participants may often hesitate to ask as learners.

The NHI's reality formation method of experience, reflection, and analysis, i.e., the "new era principle" enables Latino youth to critically examine their social realities. They isolate individual beliefs and values. They learn to choose those that work for them and to discard those that they recognize are no longer useful or even harmful. In applying this method, learners start to develop a fundamental grasp for how they can create their own realities by recognizing and challenging the social forces that influence their belief systems and shape their perspectives and perceptions. Through such insights, young Latinos also learn that they are the ultimate architects of their own social realities. They recognize that they ultimately choose for themselves and, in the process, redefine themselves, their life goals, and the pathways they prefer to follow. If they choose to turn away from remaining dependent on family, educators, or street society to define them as people and to prescribe their futures, they can choose to take the risks of exploring, experimenting, reflecting, dis-covering, and crafting their own social realities. This powerful realization serves as the foundation for self-transformation.

10.

FORMING NEW REALITIES

To remain fixed to realities that are no longer useful is to also limit our capacities to experience our new, emerging identities as a global culture.

The NHI's practice in reality formation comes from the observation of my parent's work in the 1950s, particularly in their efforts with Latino youth in the Houston barrios. Having spent years of community volunteer service with the Boy Scouts in isolated communities in the north side of Houston, they were eventually sought out by the Houston Parks and Recreation Department to run the newly constructed De Zavala Park next to the Houston ship channel. Immediately they were confronted by the challenge of providing constructive outlets for youth in a community that was characterized by marauding youth gangs, drug sales, and high dropout rates. Their most difficult challenge was in altering the prevailing community social culture that guided the behaviors and outlooks of the local residents.

With little more than an elementary school education, they transformed a community from a place where the Houston police entered with extreme caution into a thriving cultural center of youth athletics, cultural events, and civic service. Their achievements never were replicated or emulated by any other park center.

Several years later, long after their retirement and sitting in their backyard, they began talking about their years working in community development. My most immediate realization was that their efforts and the results they achieved were not accidental. They were much more than park directors responsible for planning recreational activities for the youth of the community. Instead, they were driven by a theoretical construct that they themselves crafted and followed; a plan that required hours of analysis and discussion, and, more importantly, years to implement.

Evident in their work was a vision driven by the intent to attain several important milestones. One of their goals was the construction of a culture of success to replace the operating social orientation that had defined the expectations and lifestyle of the families where they worked. They did not want the Latino youth or their families to define their aspirations by the limited environment where they lived. For my parents, economic circumstances never could be allowed to become a justification for not doing well in school or behaving in an irresponsible manner. Their second goal was to make cultural competence and pride in one's identity a compelling vision that was attractive to Latino youth. Included in this vision was for youth to make excellence a critical personal priority. By taking pride in their ethnic heritage, drawing attention to cultural imagery and celebrations, becoming proficient in Spanish and English, youth could develop a new metric to measure their place in the world. In the end, sports became the vehicle through which Latino youth began transforming themselves.

My parents firmly believed that success in athletics could have significant value in impacting the character of students and providing them the courage to stay out of trouble, finish high school and adopt a sense of responsibility towards their communities. Dad never faltered in his view towards them. To him, they were assets, inherently good in their makeup and equipped with the cultural re-sources to endure the rigors of training to compete athletically at any level in park sports activities. My mother had a much larger social notion of the com-munity. She felt that, for these youth to make significant changes in their lives, they also needed a developmental framework that involved adopting social responsibilities that extended beyond athletics.

Regardless of age, all park youth were required to register as official members. Community campaigns, conducted in cooperation with com-munity health agencies, promoted family awareness for tuberculosis and polio prevention. Door-to-door campaigns involved park youth in promoting community improvement projects such as street paving, sidewalk construction, and corner street lights for community safety. Softball leagues for all ages were organized and coached by adult community volunteers. High school girls, in addition to participating in organized sports, became members of the De Zavala Teenage Club. Annual community galas featured the coronation of the community teen queen. Sewing along with arts and crafts classes were sponsored for working parents on weekends. Younger elementary school youth participated in music appreciation, with several annually joining the children's orchestra that played at the downtown music hall. Cultural festivals were conducted with special plays on Christmas and Easter. Even older Latino men were organized into a semi-pro football league that played on Sunday afternoons.

In a short span of 10 to 12 years, De Zavala Park became the vehicle through which Santos and Esther Nieto, along with countless youth and adult volunteers were able to touch the lives of literally thousands of young men and women who lived in one of the most feared neighborhoods of Houston.

By operating on a vision that viewed the community as an asset rather than a liability; by providing families with multiple outlets for individual recognition, social ascension, and purposeful involvement; and by making the time to celebrate accomplishments; a community that once was considered to be at the bottom of Houston's social ladder had trans-formed into one of the most admired for its countless feats and accomplishments.

This fundamental understanding of community transformation served as the foundation that led to the establishment of the NHI. Somehow, my parents had found an antidote that seemed to counteract the psychological impact of poverty, of feeling powerless, and the sense of alienation that comes from being viewed as damaged or under-valued. Dad once summarized his work with my mother as "constructing a reality in which park youth could see themselves succeed."

 "They first have to witness themselves winning here before they can visualize themselves winning in anywhere else," he said one day in Spanish. "These kids already expected to lose at almost every-thing they did. We had to find ways of teaching them to win and work hard for whatever they wanted to become. The park, the softball leagues, the dances, the celebrations, the community projects, the annual banquets, the late night talks; these were ways that we used to change their ways of thinking. At the park, you could rarely lose, only win."

These conversations were both revealing and profound for me. Both of my parents understood racial discrimination but were mainly concerned with the social dynamics involved whenever two divergent cultures rivaled each other for dominance. In their view, learning to feel culturally defeated and deficient was far more dangerous and lasting than the overt expressions of racial prejudice. They saw the park as the place where young Latinos could begin healing and start learning to re-value themselves as young men and women with dignity and self-respect.

One by one, the young people of Magnolia began to change, sometimes deciding to join a park fast-pitch team or just to watch from the sidelines. They became mom's "posse" during dances, making certain that rules were observed. They stopped being menacing or picking on the younger ones, showing respect for the order and sense of organization that my parents were trying to accomplish. The simple act of no longer being violent spread to other communities, making competitions between competing teams possible. Within five years, gang violence in Magnolia ceased almost entirely. Streets became safer as did special celebrations like the annual Valentine's Day dance.

In time, DeZavala Park became the most influential and behavior-altering experience within the community. Young people finally had a place to go and play, socialize in a safe environment, and develop a sense of community pride and personal identity that lasted well into their adult lives.

The lessons of De Zavala Park were apparent in the work of the newly founded the NHI when it launched leadership programs with Latino professionals from the Austin-Central Texas area. Most were between 23 and 28 years old. These young people were ambitious and had lofty career aspirations. They already were experiencing the pressure of trying to balance two cultural worlds: one was the workplace where they were expected to dress and behave within mainstream standards and organizational culture. The other was a fading cultural environment that embraced and nurtured them as children, but now was becoming uncomfortably irrelevant and distant. They became increasingly dis-connected from their original family roots and cultural sense of identity, belonging, and membership.

In some cases, several of these young Latinos felt stuck in the middle between the two distant and often-competing worlds. They were uncomfortable because they were not able to establish or maintain a secure or enduring attachment to either environment. They neither felt White enough to fit into a dominant culture's working environments, nor Latino enough to maintain close ties to a community culture. This was the result of cultural distancing; not having the ability to speak Spanish fluently, and losing contact with former friends and extended family members. The more they actively engaged the dominant culture and its institutions, the more they became aware of the unfamiliar yet desirable opportunities that were being offered and the greater the tension they felt between their native and their host cultures.

This conflict was the topic of the conversations we had with these young professional Latinos. Four perspectives emerged.

First, the majority of believed they were caught up in a cultural flux. While they remained committed to assimilation, they also felt frustrated and dis-appointed with the required price involved in making this changeover. One such realization was marginalization in their everyday encounters at work. Some felt they were failures because they couldn't fit in with the dominant culture as they thought they should. Many placed blame on insensitive supervisors for their stalled or derailed careers. Others became suspicious and angry towards influential members of dominant culture for their biased views and ignorance of Latino culture.

Second, the older Latinos felt they had to "join the system." Their prescriptive mental model required them to try to completely assimilate in order to "beat the odds" in achieving the upward social mobility and economic success they sought.

Third, a few took the role of observers during our discussions, feeling comfortable with having attained a particular measure of social importance in their professional endeavors.

Lastly, some expressed a need to accept failure, to give up and return to their cultural roots. However, they also felt the shame of having wasted their educations and giving up on their career aspirations.

The psychological and emotional whirlwinds that were generated by the frustrations and anger expressed by these individuals did not involve questions of Latino community leadership. Rather, these individuals were too caught up in trying to settle serious inner conflicts to be strong leadership candidates. They were too concerned with changing the dominant culture, the social landscape in which they were involved to consider other outlets for their development. They only saw dead ends in their career pathways, clearly lacking the training, coaching, and mentoring that otherwise could steer them towards alternative pathways to satisfy their needs for social ascension, recognition, and sense of community purpose.

In fact, most of them felt betrayed after having fulfilled the prerequisites that were supposed to be their passports to the good life. The end result instead was alienation and feeling stuck without alternatives, except to accept the realities of their existing conditions. Undertaking the wholesale reconstruction of their individual identities entailed a cost and ensuing risk too great to pay as requirements for entering a host culture that was unwilling to change and had a poor performance record of embracing people from different cultural and racial backgrounds.

The best alternative for the NHI to fulfill our intention to broaden the supply of future U.S. Latino community leaders was to pursue younger Latinos who were not yet fully afflicted by the impact of these conflicting social influences. We believed the younger Latinos were mature enough to comprehend the implications of their social perspectives and aspirations -- even though their career goals only could be tentative at this stage of their young lives. To become future Latino community leaders, they would need to understand the dynamics of migrating between divergent cultures and navigating between dual cultural realities. They also would need to learn how to serve as influential change agents in elevating the value that Latinos collectively place on themselves as well as the value that others place on them as a community. Thus, high school age Latinos who were preparing to enter and complete college became our most likely candidates and the focus of the NHI's work that continues today.

In making this decision, the NHI determined that it could not produce the desired results simply by having young Latinos understand the dynamics and challenges of navigating the requirements of a host culture. Young Latinos of the 1980s did not have to contend with many of the barriers that previous generations had experienced. They would, however, encounter a new set of challenges that likely would be different and more draining.

As one young professional observed, "Being inside the citadel of professional society as a Latino might be considered a milestone to those who measure success by numbers, one step at a time. But those of us inside also sense the loneliness of being among the few, as well as the cost required in changing our identities to succeed."

During our first attempts in the 1980s, the NHI was marketed as a means through which academically talented young Latinos and Latinas could access top-tier national universities instead of having to settle for local community colleges. Those who attended the NHI leadership programs began shifting their college preferences to private institutions in the northeast, midwest, and California, while others gained admission to in-state flagship universities with the intent of pursuing careers in engineering, law, and medicine.

Almost immediately, we began noticing that the same concerns that occupied the thinking of their older, professional counterparts also were present among younger high school Latinos. For these students, the idea of attending college not only meant leaving home, it also meant embarking on a cultural journey from which they potentially never could return. In the view of many, leaving behind their home culture was the price that would have to be paid in order to realize their dreams of career attainment and economic security. Giving back to their local Latino communities was an afterthought they thought they might consider after they attained some level of success and importance in the larger host society. For them, acquiring the credentials to navigate in the larger world and becoming part of America's corporate infrastructure represented the best possible channels to their future successes. Leveraging their ethnicity and gender, as well as leaving home and friends, were strategies to get them to achieve success.

Between 1994 and 1998, considerable time was spent closely observing the beliefs and outlooks that appeared to be driving these young Latinos. Whether they came from California or Texas, Chicago, Houston, or New York, the inner city or rural areas, their single, most used measure of success had to do with completing college and finding employment in mainstream America. Other alternatives that potentially could define success, especially when considered from the standpoint of Latino family life and Latino communities, were never considered.

Exploring new alternatives for young Latinos to ascend socially, achieve recognition, gain a sense of importance, and develop a sense of community purpose became the focus of the NHI's work for the next several years. First, we determined that these experiences could not be conveyed through lectures and presentations. Students needed to participate in specially-crafted experiential learning opportunities with peers with whom they could share their ideas on a myriad of themes that dealt with Latino community life. They needed opportunities to compete in various social scenarios and in different settings in order to test their skills against equally competent and similarly aged peers. The more important part of these experiences was that they had to be culturally-based, so that students either could demonstrate their cultural readiness and competencies or discover voids in their development that needed attention. Finally, the NHI's game scenarios needed to provide students with the means to experience the uplifting impact of feeling important while also being recognized and applauded for their individual accomplishments by peers and family.

The insights and lessons learned in bringing these goals to fruition are too many to convey in one publication. Latino youth from California undoubtedly are different from their counterparts in Texas. There is little resemblance in the views of New Mexican and Southern Colorado youth from those in Chicago. The same can be said when comparing urban students from New York City with suburban youth from Kansas. These differences become even more apparent when international Latinos are thrown into the mix, whether they are from Panama, Mexico, or Argentina. Although together they form a fascinating mosaic of cultures that share a common language and heritage, by no means are they alike in their socioeconomic status, family education backgrounds, or outlooks.

With these differences, several conclusions can be drawn that could be important to our nation's educational and community leaders in their attempts to heighten the academic readiness of Latino youth in general and broaden the supply of well educated, highly skilled Latino community leaders in the future.

Regrettably, our public school systems currently are more concerned with the technicalities of test taking and rankings rather than engaging students in becoming aggressive self-learners. Needed in the Latino community are social entrepreneurs who are willing to establish community-based educational systems that expose both children and their parents to entirely new learning approaches and principles.

Our educational systems tend to utilize education as a means for work-force readiness. This view is reinforced by parents who share similar sentiments of education and its purpose in developing and preparing their child for successful careers. Perfectly well delineated trajectories are established for children who follow a plan of action that takes them from primary to secondary education, onward to undergraduate studies, and eventually to the work place. Children are taught to contribute to society through the type of college they intend to pursue, the majors they plan to study, and the kinds of professional jobs they wish to attain. Whether they reach these career goals or not, individuals learn to perceive and assign self-value on the basis of the work they intend to carry out and the dollar value they earn in return. Although altering these life views may be difficult, Latinos will be forced to consider alternatives simply by virtue of the growth they represent in the future and the lack of willingness by the current economic system to absorb them.

The unprecedented growth in the Latino community inevitably must be addressed. Latino families will have to assume much greater control in the education of their children, beyond the capacities of current educational systems. Entrepreneurial learning systems at community levels will be needed to prepare young Latinos to live and operate in a dual cultural reality. Being bilingual in English and Spanish not only will need to become fashionable, but expected. Developing a global mindset rather than a minority viewpoint will serve to expand a child's social references to be much more inclusive.

As changes begin to occur in the social perspectives outlooks and preferences of the Latino community so will consumer interests and purchasing habits. Fashion designs will change as will the need for more diverse preferences that also may include music, entertainment, and architecture; all of which will alter the market place and usher in an era of opportunity that will translate into larger shares of economic prosperity. These trends and directions, however, will not occur on their own. Also needed will be strong, courageous, and risk-taking Latinos who are able to envision the future and are unafraid to pursue the less traveled roads of life.

Latinos largely have been seen as a growing community of new consumers and an expanding supply source of lower-wage earners. One of the NHI's primary aims is to help break this paradigm of thought by causing a shift away from a consumer, work force driven mindset towards one of wealth-building and asset management. By guiding our youth to comprehend more fully the dynamics of consumerism and the various ways that this view engulfs and influences their operating truths, behaviors, and practices in everyday life, they also gain insight into the social forces that shape their thinking and inform the mental models they use to make important life decisions.

To remain blind to these influences and not realize the scope of their impact on the human psyche and capacities to perceive, sense, and interpret our surroundings also threatens our capacities to undergo change from within as the first step in transforming that, which surrounds us. This particular human trait is especially important to a community that is growing exponentially and promises to become one in five Americans by the year 2050. Unless the Latino community is able to equip itself with the capacities and skills to undergo change from within, becoming a significant part of tomorrow's world will mean little other than to consume in larger portions, and certainly not to participate in a larger share of the American Dream as stakeholders.

Learning to change from within will be a much more difficult proposition than attacking those whom we wish to blame for the condition of the Latino community. We must go from a reality of blaming others to a reality of taking ownership of our lives along with the responsibilities of holding ourselves accountable for our successes and failures. Rather than being rule-followers, we must learn to become rule-makers. Instead of perceiving ourselves as minorities at or near the bottom of the American social ladder, we have to adopt a world view of a global culture tied to 23 other Spanish-speaking countries of over 700 million people who all share histories, language, and customs. In other words, collectively we must endeavor to give ourselves a complete cultural makeover that ignites the imagination and energizes the human spirit.

To achieve this change in thinking and vision will not occur simply by wishing or snapping our fingers. A mechanism for community change also is needed. Third Reality as a concept and process for personal and community change was designed for this specific reason. It provides us with both a personal and community tool to assess the operating beliefs that keep us tied down to tired, worn out self-concepts of who we are as a community while fitting ourselves with new social lenses that excite imagination and makes life an exciting venture. It gives us a framework for critical self-analysis and the capacities to carefully evaluate operating beliefs that should no longer play influencing roles in the makeup of our outlooks. We also need to look at the beliefs that we consider sacred to our makeup as people, the cornerstones of our cultural heritage and richness. Finally, we need to incorporate a modern view of ourselves that looks at the future with a strong sense of excitement and anticipation. We have finally arrived at that moment in time and space when we can proudly proclaim that we have the right and capacities to shape ourselves into who we wish to be.

11.

REALITIES FOR A NEW LATINO LANDSCAPE

*Do not fear change, but whether the influences
that shape you are the designs of others
or those of your own making.*

We currently live in a world of increasing economic
uncertainty, conflicting ideologies, competing political and
economic interests, and the influences of population shifts
and trends. In the United States, wealth is being consolidated
among fewer interests. The American middle class is more at
risk economically, while new emerging populations of
Americans are facing the future with less financial assets,
cutbacks in government spending, and a redirection of public
resources. Efforts for position, power, and influence are
driven by a constant vying for skill and intelligence, which has
emerged as the new commodity for superiority among
nations.

As these interacting social forces strengthen, average working
parents are faced with making strategic choices regarding the
directions to take for themselves and their children.
Particularly at risk are Latinos. As a community, we control
the least amount of resources. We have the largest families to
support and are the least educationally prepared to move
forward. We have the least political influence, face the largest
legal battles regarding our social/citizenship status, and are
the least organizationally prepared to respond to the
challenges of the new approaching era. The stress that
Latinos face is much greater than ever before, not to mention
the consequences.

Any community that fails to develop the capacities of its youth in preparation for an emerging and shifting social landscape puts itself at risk to falling victim to the constantly changing environments of a modern day world. If we are to take stronger steps forward in galvanizing a self-sufficient community, current social models that shape our vision and understanding of the future will no longer do. In particular, the Latino community can no longer allow outside social forces to influence or determine its direction. Time, energy, thought, and dedicated effort are all necessary requirements to self-craft new priorities and directions in the future. Otherwise, we will not learn to envision and propose a direction for ourselves, or to develop the confidence needed to aggressively support our own self-crafted actions and directions.

Several key lessons can be drawn from the 32-year experience of the National Hispanic Institute, including the earlier work of my parents in Houston. Third Reality as a concept provides a framework and method to critically examine the social forces that shape who we are. It also gives us the insight needed to determine the best possible means to respond as a community to the challenges that lay ahead. Learning to examine the social forces that shape our perceptions and outlooks provide us with the means of asking ourselves pertinent questions about the preparations and directions we need to take as a community. In learning to manage social forces, we are better able to maintain focus on the goals we most wish to reach.

As a mixture of different nationalities and societal influences, Latinos must be understood according to their individual journeys and the histories of their countries of origin. U.S. Latinos, in particular, must be understood from a generational perspective. Many are third, fourth, fifth, and even seventh generation Americans who no longer have any ties to their nations of origin. Other Latinos living and working in the U.S., however, are recent immigrants. In some cases they came to the U.S. as political or economic refugees, fleeing oppressive political conditions or seeking access to jobs to satisfy basic subsistence needs for themselves and their children. Some historians have gone so far as to note that these patterns reveal little differences from the waves of other immigrant groups that have settled in the U.S. over the past centuries.

To lump these diverse and multiple cultural communities into a single category or to measure their social and economic patterns solely by income, profession, or academic attainment would be nothing less than shortsighted and a disservice. A more accurate view would be that U.S. Latinos reflect many of the same characteristics, patterns, and social trajectories as other American ethnic groups. As the education and income levels of the ethnic parents increase, the likelihood also increases that their children will subsequently succeed in school and pursue higher education. The difference for Latinos, however, has been that the patterns of income distribution and educational achievement in the U.S. have been frequently skewed in favor of certain social classes– either by custom or intent. The consequence of these practices and patterns is that those at the bottom of the economic and educational pyramid invariably reflect a greater propensity for minimal progress and repeated failure.

These were the conditions that my parents confronted in 1929 when they started as volunteers in the Latino communities of Houston. They faced similar challenges in the 1950s working with the City Parks and Recreation Department. The contrast between facilities for predominantly Latino and predominantly White communities was at best startling. Mason Park, in the southeast part of the City, was an idyllic sprawling development of nearly 100 acres of walking trails, tennis courts, in-door gymnasia, softball and baseball diamonds, clubhouse facilities for special events, and

115

an Olympic-size swimming pool for the families who lived in the surrounding community.

Fifteen blocks to the north was Magnolia, a crowded, mostly Mexican-American community where the men walked to the Houston Ship Channel to work 10 and 12-hour days loading and unloading arriving and departing ships. For this community, the City of Houston built De Zavala Park in 1951. It was a recreation area of one square city block with a tiny clubhouse that didn't have air-conditioning, a small swimming pool, and an outdoor space barely large enough to accommodate a softball diamond and dirt basketball court. My mother became the first Mexican-American to work at this community center.

Making this disparity of facilities even more glaring was that these two neighboring facilities were located only minutes from one another. It symbolized the difference in the value the elected officials at the time placed on the citizens of different but neighboring communities. It also reflected their intent to keep the two communities separated. On one hand, my mother was thrilled that the children had a new community playground. Dad held an altogether different view. He believed the reason that De Zavala Park was built was to keep Mexican-American kids from going over to Mason where the police invariably chased them off for wanting to play basketball or enjoy themselves in the swimming pool.

My parents discovered that change would not come for Magnolia's youth living in admonishing them for their behaviors or encouraging them to leave their neighborhood. Instead they designed and offered new, invigorating social realities to the community where they lived. They made participation both possible and exciting for anyone who wished to become involved. They provided them with opportunities and the means for community engagement that, in turn, allowed them to sense the feelings that invariably come from having ownership through involvement. In short, they instigated the means for both individual and community transformation, that at first was almost imperceptible. Gradually, these young people furthered their social understanding of community, improved their grades in school, excelled in high school sports, and developed meaningful career aspirations. Graduating from high school became commonplace and several attended college to pursue various professional careers. These same fundamental principles of community change were integrated into the NHI's culture and systems of beliefs and practices, with many of the same ideas continuing today, 32 years later.

The work, however, cannot continue with the sole efforts of the NHI. A new way of thinking must be developed that penetrates all institutions and touches the lives of Latino youth, starting with our public school system. By and large, our schools do good work despite the challenges of constantly changing and shifting demographics of student populations. Better pay for teachers is undoubtedly a priority as are the needs for improved state and federal academic achievement tests, and better instructional strategies that produce more and better skilled workers for an information age. Not all of the work or responsibility involved in preparing Latino youth for their futures should be seen as primarily resting on the shoulders of our nation's public school system. Small school design, charter schools, team-based training, extended school hours, improved parental involvement, better trained teacher programs, and the like are necessary to enrich the delivery of public education. As expensive and time consuming as it can become to produce new models and make improvements, attempts at educational innovation should, nevertheless, be given high priority and wholehearted support by taxpayers and private giving.

Learning experiences that provide young Latinos with the means to form realistic and healthy social perspectives, and allow them to explore different pathways for meaningful engagement in life should not be viewed as the exclusive domain of the classroom or school-sponsored extracurricular activities. Educational system leaders must see supportive learning opportunities – such as those conducted by organizations like the NHI – as legitimate avenues to advance learning both for students and their parents as well.

What educators may find interesting about the NHI's work is that learning experiences never occur in an instructional environment. Instead, students advance their intellectual and analytical capacity within environments that challenge their awareness and competencies. Through exercises in self-inquiry and introspection, students become increasingly aware and sensitive to the operating views that surround them -- some of which they come to recognize as no longer valid or useful, and potentially harmful to their individual makeup. A decluttering process occurs that leads to the incorporation of new internal frames of reference. In making these changeovers in their operating beliefs or truths, new and different starting points are introduced that compel the NHI's community of youth to pursue more relevant and purposeful options and create futures that are bright and exciting, rather than standard and conventional.

Several challenges face our public schools, especially at middle and high school levels, if they are to expand their reach into the community beyond the confinement of their campuses. The first challenge is accepting the notion that learning is not merely a cognitive exercise in human intellectual development that is restricted to teaching methods, application of national tests, and assessing youth on the basis of externally applied standards. The second challenge is in creating partnerships with legitimate, proven community organizations with the ability to create transformative learning opportunities for young people as they begin the transition from adolescence to adulthood. Without these partnerships, schools have few options to do expand a student's capacity to imagine and innovate for a 21st century society.

In the 1950s, the Houston Parks and Recreation Department provided my mother with one ball and one bat to start her first day as director. Both my parents were all too familiar with the challenges they faced. They knew about the mentality of subsistence, the incidence of crime, the widespread use of drugs, the dropout rates, the teen-age pregnancies, and the single-parent homes. They did little to focus on these problems. Rather than viewing the community from a deficit point of view, they strategically chose to identify and cultivate the assets of the youth and their families who lived there. Especially during the 1960s and the advent of the Great Society programs, De Zavala Park was routinely overlooked since it was never seen as having any serious problems that required correction or prevention. This oversight actually contributed to the successes of the park, despite Magnolia being a neighborhood that had one of the lowest income and educational levels in the entire City of Houston.

Many of the same deficit-correcting policies prevail in today's school system. Instead of funding opportunities for students who are successful in the classroom, and have the potential for making major improvements in their own lives and in their communities, the majority of our nation's resources for young people are directed mostly toward youth with serious academic and behavioral issues.

The NHI believes that success in the classroom is important, but that it is not the only measure or predictor of the future success of young Latinos. Those who do well in their academic work require much more. They need repeated

successes in other areas of human endeavor, ongoing
exposure to meaningful opportunities for personal growth
and development, and continuing involvement in learning
experiences that reinforce and reward their efforts. These
experiences allow students to challenge and retrofit their
existing beliefs, so that exploring their future selves and
striving for excellence in their development becomes a
normal expectation for them and their families.

Being able to participate in these critical learning experiences
does not come without costs. Low wage-earning families or
single parents cannot easily afford these community
experiences. Participation becomes even harder when
schools, public agencies, and private funding sources assume
that attention is best directed to those struggling to meet the
status quo, instead of those excelling academically, but in
need of leadership development. Those with the greatest
potential to contribute to their families, communities, and
American society in general become lost in the shuffle.

New views and attitudes must be formed towards youth who
endeavor to succeed, with special consideration toward
limited income populations. These youth should be rewarded
for outstanding performance that also offers them access to
community-based experiences that further their personal
growth, expand their social networks, and provide the means
of engaging in worthwhile community endeavors. To limit
their development to merely preparing for college and
entering the workplace overlooks their potential to become
valued and contributing members of a larger society. High
potential young Latinos, regardless of their ranking on social
and economic scales, require the support of private
foundations and government agencies in order to foster a
new culture of success.

Another consideration involves our nation's Latino
businesses and political and religious leaders, including the

heads of community-based organizations. Their commitment to defining social and cultural standards that measure success within a Latino perspective is crucial to the future of the Latino community. Currently, the metric most often used is an external reference whose origin lies outside of Latino community life. Oftentimes the admired and applauded Latinos are those appointed to important policy roles in government agencies or corporate firms. The tendency is to view these developments as important accomplishments, as social models for younger Latinos to consider and someday replicate. A similar frame of reference is used in measuring wealth or being elected to highly visible public roles. It defines social, economic, and political progress by transactions that take place outside of Latino community life rather than the change and benefit that occurs inwardly.

This view does not reject or criticize upwardly mobile Latinos who have found success in the mainstream of American life. Many of their accomplishments are laudable and worthy of public mention. But so, too, are the successes of Latinos who achieve success and create wealth within Latino community life. Both external and internal successes need mention in order to shape the views of future Latino leaders, especially in a Latino population that continues expanding its footprint in all aspects of American social, business, political, and government life.

Important to note is that change is already upon us and will continue to alter a landscape that once appeared to be fixed in the past. Certainly the term "minority" will no longer be a valid description of a Latino population that, before our eyes, is changing in numbers, diversity, and interests – domestically and globally. In the near future, simply completing high school and college will be inadequate to enable future generations of Latinos to navigate multiple cultures – in the U.S. and abroad.

These converging changes of a new era make it essential to redefine what it means to be Latino and to provide young Latinos with learning experiences that neither American public schools nor colleges are equipped -- or perhaps even willing -- to explore. Possibly only Latino leaders dedicated to change will commit the resources and time that will enable young Latinos to create a new realistic agenda; a new nomenclature of identity; and a new social, political, and economic landscape and world view. Failing to do so during this critical moment in history will perpetuate the depiction of Latino youth by the same worn-out measures of human value that diminish aspirations and dampen the human spirit.

The final observation comes from the years of learning and experience gained from the dedicated work of the NHI. On July 20, 2011, the NHI will celebrate over three decades of service yielding over 85,000 alumni and nearly 4,000 new participants a year, and an investment conservatively estimated at approximately $28 million over the same period. An important fact to share is that close to 97% of the funding for these initiatives over this period of time has come directly from the pockets of Latino families who strongly believe in the NHI's work and mission. We can never extend enough gratitude to a volunteer base of over 1,200 individuals every summer, not to mention the contributions of several institutions of higher learning that graciously contributed their resources to make the NHI programs possible. Institutions like Southwestern University in Texas, Austin College, and Colorado State University have been principle contributors for a remarkable span of 19 to 25 years. Similar acknowledgements go to Villanova University in Pennsylvania, the University of Rochester, and the sixty-three other colleges and universities that have invested in the NHI's talent pool of young leaders.

By participating as partners in the NHI vision, these institutions continue to make tangible contributions towards the development of young Latinos who, as potentially influential leaders, will make unique and meaningful contributions to their communities and the rest of society where they live. The continuous support that these universities show towards the NHI students demonstrates a commitment that expresses much more than simply increasing the number of Latino students who enroll as part of diversity recruiting campaigns.

An important lesson learned from working in higher education over the years is that not all colleges and universities have the same interests in Latinos or view them in the same manner. Some strive to achieve 25% representation of Latinos, not because of the human value these youth bring to their campuses, but because, in achieving this mark, they become eligible to receive extra funding from state and federal agencies. Others, where Latinos are clearly the overwhelming majority, call themselves "minority-majority institutions," as though to convey being culturally invested despite low graduation rates and high incidences of student loan forfeitures. At the other extreme are institutions that, despite being at the hub of large Latino populations, recruit only small numbers from surrounding communities. The image these institutions present is concern over losing the cultural brand that is customary to upper income families who willingly pay much higher tuition rates to give their children the privilege of being around peers from similar social and economic backgrounds.

These examples are not to alienate or make generalizations about higher education, but instead to demonstrate the nature of the challenges that face young Latinos today. The Mason Parks of the world that barred Latino youth in the 1950s were overt in their condescending treatment to outside communities. Today, changes in laws and concerns over Latino population growth obscure the reality that a disproportionate amount of Latino youth has yet to enjoy full access to the American dream. An overwhelming majority is still left to contend with scarce resources and few alternatives to pursue their life ambitions.

The NHI was fully aware of these conditions when we began our work. We recognized that progress for Latino communities could be substantially increased, but not through the continued practices of marches or in pursuing the exhausting requirements of community advocacy and reform. These strategies proved to be worthwhile in their day, but they were responses to historical conditions that may no longer capture the attention of today's Latino communities.

Similar to the work of Santos and Esther Nieto, the NHI was built on the belief and premise of seeking change from within the individual, rather than attempting to change external conditions beyond our control. We have designed learning experiences that guide young people to realize the value of navigating in an emerging and exciting global community that is interconnected by language and similarities in customs, traditions, and cultures.

By helping to develop cultural competencies and clarify individual identities, we can enable future Latino leaders to capitalize on intercultural opportunities that offer great promise and new possibilities. Our intent is for young Latinos to no longer accept the imposition of any barriers, ceilings, or boundaries regarding the range of opportunities that they can pursue. The NHI's leadership experiences help Latino youth to free themselves from self-imposed limitations and participate in shaping new social realities that infuse value in their identity and provide the space they need to participate fully in the pursuit of their individual dreams and aspirations.

Currently, the NHI's work is being catalogued and archived for future study, so the past will serve as a prologue for the construction of an expanded direction and mission. Current programs will be expanded to new regions of the U.S. and exported to additional Latin American countries. The archives will become part of the NHI's planned Centre for Leadership Development. The experience of three decades will form the basis for designing new training curricula aimed at youth workers, leaders of community civic and professional organizations, classroom teachers, school counselors, and people interested in furthering the advancement of Latino youth and Latino communities through supportive partnerships. The Centre will also provide assistance to businesses, non-profits, NGOs, and government organizations that deliver services and products to a growing Latino consumer population. More important, it will become the consultation arm for thousands of alumni who return annually to celebrate their participation with the NHI and wish to remain active members of a learning community of future Latino leaders.

At the NHI, we are excited about the new opportunities ahead. We continue to see the future with excitement, having set high expectations as an organization, while remaining true to our mission of expanding domestic and international ties with a growing community of Latino youth. The metaphor most often used in describing the impact we wish to have is of the child who is given an artist's brush and empty canvas to paint a new world of possibilities. To arrive at the new, the child must be unbiased by the past, driven by what is yet to be imagined, and armed with the cultural competence and confidence to craft daring social realities that uplift spirits, inspire imagination, and shape innovative pathways for individual and community success.

In the end, future Latino professionals face the decision between conducting life in the fast-moving lanes of competition for power and money, and being the designers and innovators of an emerging world. In the first scenario, the promise of upward mobility will undoubtedly influence those who have learned to equate success with having particular lifestyles and certain material possessions. The other option will challenge individuals to become part of a vital and evolving world of Latino culture that promises to be global in its makeup. Whatever options these future generations select, the decisions they finally reach must be their own. Once a pathway to follow is chosen, maturity and strength of character to stand by their decisions is necessary. They no longer can point at others as influencing or interfering with their right to be who they wish to become.

Transformation, however, is not an easy journey. To the contrary, it requires an almost unimaginable amount of emotional and psychological investment. It demands revealing deep, profound sentiments that often render a person vulnerable as they witness parts of themselves -- former perceptions, frameworks, and outlooks -- withering with no one around to offer comfort.

My transformational journey was sparked by my experiences working in high-level state government. I came to the slow realization that my life was irreversibly leading me to an empty destination, except in providing me with the economic wherewithal to buy a better home, eat higher quality food, drive a nice car, and maybe have a few extra dollars in the bank. The so-called benefits of middle-class America ultimately represented little value to me. Wearing nice suits, sitting in meetings, and have a title meant very little. They were all but empty water glasses that served no ultimate purpose.

Being fired at thirty-nine became an unexpected way out of a lifeless lifestyle that I hung on to for dear life. Despite the immediate anger I felt upon being asked to clear my desk, this sudden turn of events became the only way I would let go. In the end, my decision to change didn't come from this unplanned incident in my life. The confrontation was with myself, once I looked in the mirror and started asking why I was here.

If a new reality is to be constructed for a new generation of Latinos, the ideas will undoubtedly have to come from our youth. Some will question whether or not they feel the calling. Others will argue that they need a more inviting option to change from the fast track to success that they have aptly learned to navigate. Countless Latinos before have raised the same questions, many concluding that they will return back to their communities after first "making it" in the outside world.

My decision to start the long journey back actually came way before my dismissal, after a conversation with my Pop. In my early professional life, he already could see it in my eyes. He sensed my discomfort, my growing alienation. I just didn't have the guts to jump off the speeding train I was on because I didn't know what would happen or who would be there to keep me from getting hurt.

The choice was clear. I could remain where I was, already knowing what the final chapter had in store for me, or I could craft my own world, through my own initiative, my own faith, and my own willingness to stay with my decision, at any cost.

I knew all too well that in crafting a new life direction there would be no guarantees, no promises of wealth and prosperity, no assurances that the outcomes I most desired would ever be realized

I had to make my own personal journey; the journey that anyone who dares to change from within ultimately decides to take. No one can force this decision except the person willing to assume the risks involved. It was in making this decision that led my parents to do their work in Houston. It was this same decision that created the National Hispanic

Institute. Whatever mission we envisioned, whatever destination in life we wished to reach, the first step was in deciding to act without ever looking back again. The ideas had to come from our own minds and our capacity to withstand disappointments and setbacks. We had to rely on our God-given capacities to craft, invent, and innovate. Imagination, faith and the will to act were by far the most important elements in our individual quests.

Future leaders can never represent themselves to the Latino community as if they have the answers that others do not. Individuals who wish to play influential roles must learn to become influencers of change, adept at asking questions, and able to analyze and synthesize community responses in pursuit of the highest forms of collaboration. No longer needed are top-down hierarchies of decision making that serve the interests of those not invested in community. Patience and carefully thought- through approaches must replace expediency in community engagement and development.

Above all other consideration is the decision to deeply engage in Latino community a life. Part-time or weekend leadership will no longer suffice for a community that will represent one in five Americans in the not too distant future. It will be essential to incorporate a culture of success that is expectation-driven, rather than the therapeutic, intervention approach that has been in play since the 1960s. Being Latino should become a destination and a point of reference that generates genuine interest and involvement. It cannot be an exit gate for those who use their ethnicity to leverage their circumstances. Our leaders of the future must possess a deep, sacred trust in Latinos that extends beyond personal interest and is non-negotiable to the ever-present influences of outside interests.

For those daring enough to want a different outcome for the Latino community, these same choices apply. The calling sound of sirens will always be there, promising a richer life for those with degrees, titles, and careers as the promise and lure of a better life.

I was there, knowing all too well what those sounds and promises meant. In my case, I no longer paid attention. I also know that they exist today for those who want to follow them like the deer responding to mating calls of a waiting hunter. The question young Latinos must ultimately face is not whether those options exist for them. It is in deciding which path they will take in becoming the people who they wish to be.

AFTERWORD

How does the world begin anew?

The question swirls in our minds, driven by a desire to venture and a penchant for gain. It clicks at our ears, rattling our fears of mediocrity and shaking us from our slumber. It eats at our food and steals its taste, until our ultimate discovery: we are the builders.

It was decided long ago, when we first snatched glimpses of tomorrow. We couldn't unsee the gardens, the kingdoms of our making; we couldn't untaste the freedom in our kneaded bread. Circumstance left blueprints in our character, designs in our line of vision. We couldn't unhear the compositions. They settled in our bellies and grew up our spines, leaving blooms of harmony for our heads to rest. It was then that our fates were sealed.

We are the builders, the bringers of the world to come. Our memories are filled with smooth mud-brick and scrolls of our visions. We cast iron for ourselves and carve ebony for our families. We raise schools for our teachers and homes for our children. The fruits of our labor bring bread to our baskets. But we must choose what we build.

Haphazard roads are before us, trailed by cold hammers and needy nails with laid out plans of distant castles. The rewards of these towers run hard: our baskets will be full, but the kingdom will not be ours. Some choose to become masons for their majesties. They tuck away the scrolls of their making and attempt to unsee the gardens of their snatched glimpses. They need bread, they say. But we, the builders of our domain, must craft. We stay.

So we begin. Leaving behind promises of full bounties and faraway majesties, we take up arms in pursuing our purpose. We are the builders, the breadmakers, the composers. The creators of our kingdom. Our cast iron, hearty dough, and strong melodies are the fruits of our making. We simply take to our blueprints, the designs in our line of vision, and lay our first modest bricks. We begin the world anew.

Alexandria Ocasio-Cortez, NATLDZ 2005
Boston, Massachusetts, Summer 2010

72626460R00074

Made in the USA
Columbia, SC
22 June 2017